Strange Gods

Strange Gods

Responding to the Rise of Spirit
Worship in America

by

Keith M. Bailey

CHRISTIAN PUBLICATIONS, INC.
CAMP HILL, PA

Christian Publications, Inc.
3825 Hartzdale Drive, Camp Hill, PA 17011
www.cpi-horizon.com

Faithful, biblical publishing since 1883

ISBN: 0-87509-770-7

Cover Photos by Richard Dellinger
and Corel Stock Photos

Unless otherwise noted, Scripture taken from
the New King James Version.
© 1979, 1980, 1982
by Thomas Nelson, Inc., Publishers.

This book
is dedicated to the
Native American Christians
who have so greatly
enriched my life.

Contents

Foreword...xi

Introduction...1

One • *What Is Animism?* 9

Although animism (the worship of evil spirits) is as old as our fallen race, well over one-half of the world's population today are animists, including many educated and prosperous people in North America. The Christian community must reach out in love to a lost world while affirming the fact that Christ is the only way.

Two • *Spirit Worship—Then and Now* ... 27

Until this century, the practice of animism in America was looked upon as deviant and dangerous. But now pluralism is considered by some as a legitimate form of faith. Historic Christianity cannot go along with this trend. The Church must reach out to a lost world while insisting and affirming that Christ is the only way.

Three • *A Biblical View of Animism* 51

Modern anthropology has made extensive studies of animism in many parts of the world. Although these resources provide valuable information as to the observable aspects of this religious system, only the Old Testament gives an overview of the practices of animism in the ancient world. The

New Testament affirms that in Christ every provision for victory has been made.

Four • *Deliverance Ministry among Native Americans* 77

Despite a lengthy history of practice and culture rooted in spirit worship, Native Americans are finding freedom from spiritual bondage in Christ. Those who minister to animistic peoples must be able to discern which activities are rooted in darkness. If our sense of spiritual bondage is less than biblical, we will fail in our mission.

Five • *The Powerful Effects of Revival* 101

Today, as the evangelical Church faces the task of evangelizing the great diversity of animistic people now residing in America, there will undoubtedly be many cases of deliverance. Controlling demonic forces must be challenged before the harvest can be gathered in. Deliverance is sometimes a significant dimension of evangelism.

Six • *Ten Biblical Principles for Effective Deliverance Ministry* 123

The Word of God provides an objective and factual view of the hosts of hell and affirms that all believers may experientially and victoriously confront these dark forces because of Christ's triumph over them. Christians do best in battle when they appropriate basic biblical principles and take their place beside the winner—Christ Jesus, the Lord.

Seven • *Preparation for the Battle* 155

The resurgence of animism in this century in so-called Christian countries of the world is a clear call to the Church to offer deliverance to the captives in Christ's name. Only a pure, Spirit-empowered Church can triumphantly confront the domain of deception, darkness, demons, death and damnation.

Eight • *Sorting It Out, Keeping on Track* 175

Fundamental to a sound ministry of deliverance is a sound theology of deliverance. It is time to sort out the various theories, methodologies and secular intrusions into detecting and overcoming demonic activity, and to reaffirm the theological and biblical basis of the deliverance ministry. Such a stance will keep us from drifting toward the fanatical fringe in matters of spiritual warfare.

Nine • *The Church's New Battlefront* 199

For the first time in the modern era, the Church in the West is faced with a sizeable population of people who worship evil spirits. The alarm has been sounded. This battle with strange gods will require a Spirit-filled Church armed with sound doctrine, the integrity of holiness and a view to the glory of God at His ultimate victory.

Appendix A • *Demon Possessed
or Demonized?* 221
Appendix B • *Territorial Spirits* 229
Appendix C • *The Generational
Transmission of Demons* 237
Bibliography 241

Foreword

WE ARE LIVING in a day of heightened interest in things relating to the Native American both in secular and spiritual realms. It has commonly been accepted that the Native American experience has been one of a spiritual journey. Everywhere one turns there are documentaries, movies, books and crafts espousing all things Native.

As Native Americans, we are keenly aware of this growing interest in the affairs of our people and the impact it is having on society as a whole. We also realize that hidden behind the media portrayals of our ways looms the dark, fearful side of encounters and dealings with the supernatural. Dr. Keith Bailey has provided the Church of Jesus Christ with an important and significant tool in dealing with the powers of the unseen world.

Most Native American people who read this book will no doubt be able to affirm the things of which it speaks. In fact, one of us (Herman Williams) was an eyewitness to some of the experiences included here. And we both could provide many other examples from our combined ministries among our people that would confirm the truths so powerfully related.

Dr. Bailey is highly respected for his life and work among us. His love and advocacy for Native Americans has given him a special place as a wise and true elder. His mastery of our language, his firsthand knowledge of the spirit world and his understanding of the complexities and concerns of Native people as it relates to gospel ministry give him the qualifications to speak of the issues he raises in this book.

We count it a great privilege to know Dr. Bailey as a true counselor, spiritual leader and friend. We wholeheartedly commend this book both to our own people and to the whole body of Christ as a resource in understanding and dealing with the darker side of animistic practices.

Rev. Herman J. Williams,
Navajo Pastor

Rev. Craig S. Smith,
Chippewa Evangelist

Introduction

AGENERATION AGO only anthropologists and overseas missionaries talked about animism or, as it is more commonly known, the worship of evil spirits. To the average Western Christian, animism had no relevance.

But with the events of the past two decades, the consideration of animism is no longer irrelevant. It is now a hot topic among knowledgeable North American Christians. The revival of paganism coupled with the migration of numerous animistic people groups to our shores has made encounters with animism almost a daily occurrence.

An evangelical pastor in a Midwestern city was called to the home of an elderly lady to work out her funeral arrangements. A grandson of the deceased asked the pastor if he could have a part in the funeral. The pastor asked the young man what he had in mind. Without hesitation, he said that he wished to perform a Native American purification ritual consisting of burning sweet grass to ward off evil spirits. The pastor explained that he could not allow such an ceremony as part of a Christian burial service.

The day of the funeral the pastor noticed the young man waiting some distance from the grave until all the people left. Thinking he was alone, he then proceeded to place incense on the grave and perform the animistic rite. It was later learned that this young man from a Christian family had been led into animism by a backslidden believer. This kind of experience brings the impact of the new animism very close to home.

Recently I received a telephone call from a Christian man whose wife renounced Christianity and embraced Native American spirituality New Age style. The man was almost beside himself with anguish as he explained what this was doing to their marriage and their home. He told me that although his wife was raised in a Christian home and attended church all her life, she had begun to lose interest. Before long she was reading New Age material and researching Native American religion.

Her search took her to Colorado to a retreat where people were seeking to contact the spirit world by means of fetishes. The husband's alarm increased when she announced her intention to place shaman-blessed fetishes throughout their home. At this point, the Christian husband took a stand and refused to allow the fetishes in the house.

Incidents such as the one just described will become more and more common in the future. Ministers who in the past have not had to deal with this form of power encounter or any form of demonic activity cannot now avoid the effects of this animistic invasion of our land and culture.

Animism is no longer largely confined to the Third World. It has always been present in the West, but now it has come on a massive scale and must be reckoned with by the Church. In the future, evangelism and discipleship in Western churches must take into account the problems of making converts from among animists.

Animism has changed facades many times across the ages but it is fundamentally the same as it was immediately after the fall of man. The worship of evil spirits has been and still is a major world religion. The Church in the West, especially the Protestant Church after the Reformation, has ignored that fact for centuries, but the circumstances of the modern world demand that we reckon with this reality.

The teachings of Christ and the New Testament Scriptures as a whole make abundantly clear that He expected His Church to do battle with the powers of darkness right down to the day of His coming. He ascended on high having amply provided for the offensive and defensive aspects of this war. He Himself is the Captain of the hosts of the Lord and shares His great Calvary victory with His people. The conflict of the ages is not just an interesting theological idea. It is a reality with which every serious Christian must come to terms.

In the past, the Church in America and other Western nations has had a comfort zone between them and the spirit worship that characterizes the religious practices of so many peoples of the world. The decline of true spirituality in the Church, together with the massive population shifts resulting from war in other parts of the world, has produced a sizable animistic presence in the so-called Christian countries.

In the United States, animism was once confined to Native American reservations and small pockets of the occult activity which included theosophy and the Spiritualist Church. This cult, started in the eighteenth century, is devoted to making contact with the dead. Today animism is mainstream, with Madison Avenue-style television advertising luring the unwary to try psychic readings to solve their problems. These slick ads are designed to make this misadventure into the world of the supernatural appear legitimate. And television documentaries are devoted to eulogizing Native American animism, betraying the promoters' preoccupation with material related to the occult or various forms of animism.

One popular prime-time show presents a frontier lady doctor and her encounters with Native American religion. Ceremonies used by Indian medicine men appear as beautiful religious expressions with no hint that the purpose of these rituals is to contact evil spirits. Another long-running television program was built on animistic practices of the Far East, the hero frequently engaged in out-of-body experiences and the demonstration of occult powers.

Most newspapers in American cities publish a religious page at least once a week with articles about special events sponsored by the churches of the community. These pages are no longer exclusively used for Christian churches, but include information on events in Islamic, Buddhist and even occult groups. Our local paper recently interviewed the pastor of a spiritualist church who in answering questions about the teaching of his church identified it with the New Age movement.

In many American cities the drums and rattles of Native American ritual can be heard on weekends as Indians gather to maintain and perpetuate their traditional ways in the midst of modernity.

A pastor in New York City shared his experience in establishing a church among the Haitian population of that metropolitan area. Most of his congregation were recent immigrants to the United States. He found that at least one-fourth of them were possessed by evil spirits as a result of their association with voodooism in their native country. A large portion of his time became devoted to the ministry of deliverance.

The time has come when the evangelical Church in the United States must learn to minister in a culture where animism is a significant force. To meet this challenge, the Church needs a fresh outpouring of the Holy Spirit. Spiritual warfare can no longer be just a curiosity considered academically by comfortable Christians. Such warfare is vital in dealing with this present resurgence of paganism.

The positive side of the current situation is the possibility that the Church may recover its understanding of the great gap between good and evil. It may once again stand bold in its allegiance to the Lord Jesus Christ and with uncompromising commitment wage war against the powers of darkness in His exalted name.

This book has been written with the prayer that it may be a useful resource for God's people when they encounter the powers of darkness in any forum. The material has been field-tested by more than fifty years of prayer, study and actual deliverance ministry among animistic people and others. I have learned from these disciplines and experiences the absolute, unchanging power of Christ.

The Bible has shown itself true in every instance. The Holy Spirit works today just as He did in the first-century Church. Biblical Christianity is not a thing of the past. It has the answer when all human methodologies have failed. Christ is ready for the present-day renewal of animism. He waits for us to trust Him and to believe His Word.

What Is Animism?

Although animism (the worship of evil spirits) is as old as our fallen race, well over one-half of the world's population today are animists, including many educated and prosperous people in North America. The Christian community must reach out in love to a lost world while affirming the fact that Christ is the only way.

THE TERM "ANIMISM" made its debut in the late nineteenth century in the writings of E.B. Tyler. His book *Primitive Culture*, written from a secular viewpoint, uses the word "animism" for the forms of spirit worship this scholar discovered among primitive people.[1] It ultimately became a part of the nomenclature of the new, developing discipline of anthropology in which anthropologists applied the term to the activity and worship of spirits among peoples in many parts of the world.[2]

Animism is first of all a religious system, but it is also a philosophical system which supplies its followers with a worldview. Animists believe that spirits indwell all animate and inanimate objects.[3] Even those animists who believe in one superior Creator-God worship the spirits and not the Creator-God. Animists sometimes distinguish between what they perceive to be good or evil spirits. Scholars have also correctly called animism a medical system whereby the followers depend upon the spirit world in their battle with sickness and disease.

The practice of animism is not the exclusive domain of so-called primitive people. Well over one-half of the world's population are animists, including many educated and prosperous people. The great ethnic religions of the world—Islam and Buddhism—display strong undercurrents of animism. A high percentage of the adherents of these two religions are practicing animists. The late veteran missionary Samuel Zwemer observed that Islam and Buddhism have never been able to overcome animism in their converts.[4]

This comment is important in light of the intense Islamic effort to evangelize in America. Beautiful mosques and Islamic centers are being erected by the hundreds across the United States. Millions of dollars are being spent by the Muslim world to penetrate the West with their message.[5]

While much of the information regarding animism in this book comes from firsthand knowledge of animism as practiced by Native American tribes, the reader should understand that animism in our country and around the world includes the followers of many religions both ancient and modern.

Though Islam and Buddhism have failed to free their converts from animism, the Church of our Lord Jesus Christ has a far different record. Millions have been liberated from the bondage, fear and darkness of animism through the power of Christ. Deliverance from the spirits has, since the dawn of Christianity, been a sign that the kingdom of God is manifest. Jesus said to the critical Pharisees, "But if I cast out demons by the Spirit of God, surely the kingdom of God has come upon you" (Matthew 12:28).

Following the teaching of Christ, the Church has determined that the spirits worshiped by animists are evil spirits or demons. The truth of this position will become more obvious as we examine the nature of animism and the effects it has upon those who believe and practice it.

Examples of Animism

Animism among Native Americans

The nature of animism can best be understood by examining an actual animistic religion such as the Grand Medicine native to the Ojibwa Indians in Canada and the United States. Basic to their belief is the concept that every animate or inanimate object is indwelt by a spirit who is to be feared, worshiped and, when necessary, appeased. All of life is touched by this teaching. If one goes fishing and makes a catch, offerings must be given to the spirits that dwell in the lake or stream from which the fish came. When a man cuts down a tree for firewood, an offering is left for the spirit that dwells in the tree. The many offerings given the spirits often drain the worshipers' already limited resources.

They also believe that the spirits communicate with the ancestors of the tribe. An elaborate system with complicated protocol characterizes this particular form of animism. Out of fear of reprisal, its followers give expensive sacrifices to the spirits whose duty it is to see that their sacrifices are taken to the spirit world and given to the donors' ancestors. The sacrifices often consist of clothing, food or whiskey—anything the person liked in this world.

Dances and songs become the vehicle of communication with the spirits. Many elaborate rituals must be performed to please the *manidoog* (Chippewa for "spirits"). Considerable time, effort and money are needed to carry out the ceremonies. In the Grand Medicine there are various kinds of shamans, all of whom have special powers for which they have made compacts with the spirits. Through fasting and prayer they receive the power to curse, to heal, to find lost objects, to defeat enemies and to perform other supernatural acts. They are therefore feared by the people. They sometimes even use their powers against each other, often resulting in death for the "loser" in the conflict.

Young men do not join the Grand Medicine until they have a dream or vision revealing their mediator. It could be a bear, a bird, a deer or objects associated with animals. A bear's claw or a deer tail could become their *chibig* (charm) which they carry on their person and consider very sacred. The *chibig* is used as their medium to communicate with the spirit world.

The animists that I have known did not consider the spirits to be kind, loving and merciful, but viewed them as creatures of darkness. The thought of displeasing them sent terror to their souls, for the spirits were believed to have unlimited power. They must therefore be appeased at any cost. Animists live on the edge of the supernatural. The presence and power of the spirits is obvious to them and their help is sought for hunting, fishing, planting and about everything else they do. They literally live under the shadow of the spirit world.

There is a wide gap between the actualities of animism and the television documentaries on the subject. Time does not permit a study of the many forms of animism in the Native American scene. However, it should be noted that the Sun Dance of the Dakotas, the Longhouse of the Six Nations and the Medewigan of the Chippewas, while appearing to be very different, are really the same at their core. Each of these idolatrous religious systems advocate the worship of gods who embody the powers of darkness.

The neglect of the American Church to evangelize the Native American is a blot on the record of a Church that has generally excelled in world evangelism. The neglect of the Church, coupled with a lack of integrity on the part of government in dealing with Native Americans, has driven them to a renewal of their traditional animistic religions. A growing number of Native American intellectuals, disillusioned by the mistreatment of their people, tend to romanticize those religions.

Television specials on this subject, prepared by Native Americans, generally emphasize what they perceive to be the environmental issues of their religions. They see the earth as their mother and present their religion as an innocent attempt to live in harmony with nature. This interpretation goes well with liberal thinking and those who accept religious pluralism as a noble achievement. But it does not measure up to the facts. To ignore the animistic base of Native American religions is to be dishonest with the facts.

Having said this about the traditional religion of our Native American friends, let me also say that they are an intelligent and noble people. It was my privilege to live for ten years on a Native American reservation and to work daily with them. My understanding of their culture was also greatly enhanced through the learning of three tribal languages. As a people they have much to offer other cultures. Having Native American friends for over forty years, I can testify to the enrichment they have brought to my life. To point out the animistic nature of Native American religion is not intended to be derogatory. The fact of spirit worship among them can be verified by Native Americans themselves.

Animism is not peculiar to the native population of North America but is found in every part of the world. In fact, even the most sophisticated Western nations have practicing animists. It is ancient and it is worldwide. Modern anthropology has sometimes represented animism as a step in the evolution of monotheistic religion.[6] However, anthropologists have uncovered artifacts that call into question this theory. There is substantial evidence that monotheism was first and animism came later.[7] The Bible clearly shows animism to be a product of the fall of man and his rebellion against God the Creator (Romans 1:18-21).

Animism among Immigrants

After the fall of Vietnam to the communists, a

stream of Asian immigrants fled to the United States and other Western countries. Thousands of tribespeople came to America from Laos, Cambodia and other parts of Southeast Asia. Among them were the Hmong, who for centuries had been an oppressed people, living in underdeveloped areas and carrying on the traditional lifestyle inherited from their ancestors.

The Hmong respect two kinds of spirits—those who indwell the trees, mountains, waterfalls, rivers, valleys and other natural objects, and the household spirits who are the spirits of the dead from their immediate family.

Although coming from primitive life in the jungles, the Hmong are a very intelligent and industrious people who have adapted well to Western culture. In the matter of just a couple of decades they have carved out a place for themselves in America.

Remarkable and successful evangelism has taken place among the Hmong. At this writing, The Christian and Missionary Alliance alone has seventy-eight North American congregations with an inclusive membership of over 18,000.[8] Rev. Timothy Vang, who for several years had oversight of these churches, points out that with the traditional religion of the Hmong being animistic the Church often faces the demonic in her efforts to evangelize her own people. The following account is adapted from material he shared with me. You will note the basic similarities between this form of animism and others we have described: the characteristic use of shamans, offerings to the spirits, the belief that spirits indwell objects and people, fear of the spirits and demonic possession.

Animism among the Hmong People

During the New Year's celebration the leaders of the village go to the tallest mountain or the tallest tree to present offerings to their gods. The offerings usually include a live chicken (which will be killed at the site), some cooked rice and incense. The request is made that the spirit which indwells the tree or the mountain protect the village for the coming year.

The Hmong believe that the tiger is indwelt by spirits. If a person is sick, very tired, unable to eat and drink and does not respond to medicine, they assume he or she is targeted by a tiger for death. The tigers, they believe, sometimes sleep with the sick during the night. Footprints outside the house often substantiate this belief. When daylight comes, the tiger escapes to the jungle.

Animal sacrifices are made to the spirits according to the instructions of the shaman. If a person is sick, the shaman is called to perform a healing ceremony which the Hmong call *uaneneg*. The shaman will cover his face with a black apron and put on fingerbells, shaking them to make noise. He then goes into a trance. While in the trance, he begins to sing, calling the spirits of the *neng* to lead him to the world beyond where he will seek the lost spirit. When he finds it in the hands of the evil spirits, he bargains for the release of the lost spirit. After the ceremony is finished, the shaman advises the head of the household as to what animal has been bargained—a chicken, pig, cow or water buffalo. Once the family has secured the animal, the shaman returns for the final ceremony.

Once, when I was a boy, I was helping the family clear a space in the jungle for a plantation. At lunchtime, my father took some food—rice, meat and vegetables—and walked a distance from the family. He then looked to the surrounding mountains and said, "Oh, you spirits of the mountains, the valleys and the trees, I beseech you to come and eat with me. I ask you to protect me and my family as we work here today."

During New Years, the head of the household is forbidden to eat until he has made offerings to the spirit of the house first. When the meal of chicken and pig is cooked, he takes a bowl of new rice and a bowl of boiled meat and places them on a table inside the house. He then puts several spoons in the bowls and begins speaking to the spirits. The head of the house calls the grandparents, parents, brothers, sisters and children that have died to come and eat. After calling the spirits of the dead, he himself will eat.

During healing ceremonies, the shamans cast out demons. This is done only for those who are terminally ill. When the family believes the patient is possessed by evil spirits, two or more shamans are called to perform the ritual. The cost for this ceremony is about $150 U.S.

While the family is chanting, a shaman will hit the house with a peach tree stick to drive out the evil spirits. The Hmong believe that only a young peach tree limb will cause the demons to fear. At this point in the ritual, the shaman fills his mouth with boiling pork grease. He then runs here and there in the house spewing the hot oil on the walls and floors to chase the spirits out.*

The Hmong initiate their children into spirit worship at infancy. On the third day after a child is born, they kill an animal (chicken, cow, pig or water buffalo depending on the wealth of the family). Members of the clan gather in the house to choose a name for the child. A ceremony called *huplee* is performed to call a spirit into the child, a spirit that will be his or her personal spirit. If that spirit wanders about or is captured by the evil spirits, the child will be ill and need the healing ceremony.

---

*   When I was a boy, a school friend was passing a house when the shaman spewed the hot oil and it burned the boy's hair. However, the boiling pork oil did not burn the mouth of the shaman.

After the child is given a name and receives a spirit, he belongs to the clan and must obey its religious rituals. If a girl marries into another clan, she is released from the ritual of her clan. Hmong women cannot marry within their own clan. The men, however, remain in their original clan to assume the family leadership when the fathers die. Men bear the responsibility to care for the household spirits and please the spirits outside the family by making the appropriate sacrifices.

Each clan among the Hmong have their own rituals. The Vang clan is divided into the "Vang Hmong" and the "Vang Chinese." An interesting legend accounts for the two clans. Once when the Hmong were fleeing China, they arrived at a place where there were many graves. Ordinarily, when the Chinese buried, they put lines of stone on the grave while the Hmong did not. Often when the Chinese would find Hmong graves they would dig them up and expose the bodies to the sun which was a great disgrace to the Hmong.

One group of Hmong decided to put

the lines on their graves so the Chinese would not dig them up. That group of Hmong are called the "Vang Chinese." The group that escaped from China did not follow the Chinese burial practice and are known as the "Vang Hmong." There are eighteen clans of Hmong from Laos now living in the United States.[9]

Animism in the Past

The worship of evil spirits is as old as our fallen race. When Adam fell into sin the door was opened for demonic activity in the human experience. Immediately the mercy of God provided a way of true worship based on atonement and forgiveness. But not all of Adam's posterity elected to worship the true God. Yielding instead to their fallen natures, they worshiped evil spirits. The Old Testament offers ample proof of this traffic with the demonic.[10]

As the world's population grew and scattered over the earth, spirit worship sprang up among all the nations. Extensive worldwide animistic worship is not a new condition, but goes back to the dawn of history.[11] Scripture consistently condemns the practice of spirit worship in all of its forms (Isaiah 8:19-20). The moral order established by God our

Creator forbids the worship of any other gods (Exodus 20:3). Demons, however, like their master the devil, crave the worship of human beings (Matthew 4:9). Their hold on mankind is basically religious (1 Timothy 4:1). The strategy of the powers of darkness centers on ensnaring the souls of fallen people in the false worship of the demons (2 Corinthians 4:3-4).

Animism was prevalent in the Old Testament world. It was the practice of animism that brought the judgment of God on the Canaanites (2 Chronicles 33:1-9). The law of God strictly prohibited the practice of animism in Israel. In Deuteronomy 18:9-14, Moses instructed Israel as to the nature of animism, showing that it is an abomination to the Lord, as are all those who practice it (18:12). Moses, under the direction of the Holy Spirit, gives God's people a breakdown of and warning about the various forms of animism practiced in Canaan and the surrounding nations: They were to avoid soothsayers, witchcraft, sorcery, mediums, conjurers of spells and the passing of children through the fire.

In the next chapter, "The Practice of Spirit Worship Then and Now," we will evaluate the significance of these warnings for us presently and in the future should the Lord delay His coming.

Endnotes

[1] Bronislow Malinowski, *Magic, Science and Religion* (Boston: Beacon Press, 1948), p. 1.

[2] Edward Clodd, *Animism, the Seed of Religion* (London: Archibald Constable and Co., 1905), p. 26.

[3] Ibid., p. 42.

[4] Samuel Zwemer, *The Influence of Animism on Islam* (MacMillan Company, 1920), p. 6.

[5] George Otis, Jr., *The Last of the Giants*, (Tarrytown, NJ: Fleming Revell, 1991), p. 62.

[6] Simon Coleman and Helen Watson, *An Introduction to Anthropology* (New Jersey: Chartwell Books, 1990), p. 93.

[7] Malinowski, *Magic,* p. 7.

[8] *Annual Report to the General Council of The Christian and Missionary Alliance,* 1996, p. 77.

[9] Excerpted from letter dated March 14, 1996, from Rev. Timothy Vang.

[10] Robert Brown, *Demonology and Witchcraft* (London: John F. Shaw and Company, 1889), p. 7.

[11] Ibid., p. 14.

CHAPTER TWO

Spirit Worship —Then and Now

Until this century, the practice of animism in America was looked upon as deviant and dangerous. But now pluralism is considered by some as a legitimate form of faith. Historic Christianity cannot go along with this trend. The Church must reach out to a lost world while insisting and affirming that Christ is the only way.

ONE MIGHT ASK what relevance these ancient practices have to modern life. The practices of spirit worship today follow these same forms. There is nothing new about the "New Age." It is the same spiritual corruption that devastated the Canaanite culture 4,000 years ago. This false worship characterized Sodom and Gomorrah (Genesis 13:13). No matter what cultural levels these civilizations reached, their deviation to the worship of spirits in time destroyed their culture.[1] There seems to be a pattern in the ancient world that the widespread practice of animistic religion precipitated the decay and downfall of those nations.[2]

Until this century, the practice of animism in America was looked upon as deviant and dangerous, carried on for the most part underground.[3] But in the last decade it has come into the open. American culture is becoming more and more ac-

cepting of animism as a norm. The devotees of religious pluralism now consider animism a legitimate form of faith.[4] Some universities offer
witchcraft as a course of study.[5] The media and
some journalists exalt the animist as a model of
sincerity, offering hope to our culture. Such naivete
among intelligent people is astounding. The cold
hard facts have been ignored in favor of a romantic
idealism grounded in an irrational, pluralistic view.
The situation presents a serious challenge to the
Church of God.

Academia is telling society that animism is not
the bad thing we once thought it to be, but instead
is a possible breakthrough to new spiritual hori-
zons. Nothing could be farther from the truth than
that assumption. When the true nature of animism
is understood, it will be seen as a threat to Western civilization and to the Church. The clear teaching of the Bible is that animism is satanic in origin
and is basically the worship of dark and deceiving
demons.

The contemporary Church is not well prepared
to address this problem. For most of our history
the Church in the West has ignored demonology,
assuming that it was a problem only in other parts
of the world. Missionaries made references to it,
but the average pastor knew nothing about demonology and did not see it as relevant to pastoral

care. The current situation across our nation challenges that viewpoint. Thousands of animistic people from all parts of the world have now arrived on American shores, bringing with them the tradition of spirit worship.

The Church needs to ready herself both to evangelize and disciple animists. Many new immigrants live in bondage to a system of diabolical deceptions and can only be freed by the all-powerful work of Jesus Christ. They are reachable, as can be demonstrated by successful missionary work in any number of Third World countries where animism is the dominant religion. The West African nations of Congo, Mali and Gabon, among others, have witnessed the conversions of thousands of animists.

The rapid growth of ethnic churches being formed in America from largely animistic people is phenomenal. Fortunately, pastors from animistic cultures are leading these churches and understand the problems of discipleship one encounters in this work. But not all of the new immigrants have access to churches sensitive to their ethnic origins. The average Anglo-American church has the responsibility to reach out to these people in their communities. Such an undertaking brings with it a direct engagement in spiritual warfare.

Evangelistic endeavor will be the first battlefield of this war. The forces of darkness will assemble their emissaries to combat the effort to win souls among those who worship the powers of darkness. The demons will not be passive. The Church must rally her forces and put on the whole armor of God. No human methodology will defeat the forces of hell. This is a supernatural war requiring God's people to lay aside their twentieth-century religious playthings and lay hold of the power of God through Spirit-energized prayer.

Religious pluralism is a major challenge to historic Christianity in our time. We dare not allow ourselves to be deceived as to the nature of this conflict. Neither syncretism nor compromise can be tolerated. If we are to present with integrity the gospel of Christ to the animists in this country we must be prepared for an all-out battle with the powers of darkness. The Church's walk, work and warfare must demonstrate the absolute triumph of the Lord Jesus Christ over all the powers of hell.

The malignant powers specialize in deception. Every effort will be made to make religious pluralism acceptable. Discerning Christians will see past the facade that attempts to paint animism as a simple, beautiful religion worthy of consideration as an answer to some of the dilemmas of modern man. The Greek religion of Paul's day illustrates this danger (Acts 17:22-23). The advanced civilization of the Greeks seems to argue for the legitimacy of their religious system until one examines its true nature. Coneybeare and Howson in their classic work on the writing and times of the apostle Paul make the following observation on Greek religion:

> If in any region of Heathendom the evil spirits had pre-eminent sway, it was in the mythological system of Greece, which, with all its beautiful imagery and all its ministrations to poetry and art, left man powerless against his passions, and only amused him while it helped him to be unholy. In the lively imagination of the Greeks the whole visible and invisible world was peopled with spiritual powers or demons. The same terms were often used by Pagans and by Christians. But in the language of the Pagan the demon might be either a beneficent or a malignant power: in the language of the Christian it always denoted what was evil.[6]

Ancient Greek culture was brilliant in literature, art and philosophy but bankrupt in morality. That does not necessarily mean that evil spirits are the force behind great literature and art. It does mean that the forces of darkness can and will promote such a rich culture if it is kept amoral. Evil spirits are the prime movers behind unholiness. Satan will do all he can to make his product look respectable on the surface while underneath there is nothing but wickedness. The enemy of our souls always works behind a slick facade. God's people need to develop discernment so as not to be deceived by the devil's attractive charade used to hide the moral poison that is boiling out of the spirit world.

Animism, American Style

Perhaps the most dangerous form of spirit worship is the new Westernized version of animism: the New Age movement. It uses the popular concepts of environmentalism to give it respectability. The chief promoters of the New Age are often celebrities in the arts or entertainment world. They do not hesitate to use the public forum to propagate their teaching. The media publicizes their meetings and rituals.[7] Secular bookstore chains inventory shelves full of books on the occult and the New Age. Personal observation reveals that the occult literature section in secular bookstores is often larger in volumes than the offerings of Christian books. Westernized animism is coming on in full color with all the technological power it can muster.

The New Age—an Old Lie

The New Age movement is aggressively anti-Christian and openly attacks the basic doctrines of the Christian faith.[8] While claiming to be a kind of spirituality that will usher in a new age for the world, it has nothing to offer but ancient forms of animism. What is new about pantheism? Or the transmigration of souls? Channeling has been around for centuries. And transcendental meditation is nothing new.

The New Age worldview is essentially that held by pagans around the world. It is a mixture of Eastern religions, psychology, Native American religion and ancient pagan religions from many parts of the world. It is the inevitable outcome of religious pluralism. But those who look to religious pluralism for the needs of their soul will find only a deep, dark and empty hole. There is nothing there to fill the void of a lost soul.

The New Age religion practiced by modern sophisticated Americans is nothing more nor less than animism, and God condemns animism. In the days ahead, many disillusioned souls caught up in this diabolical system will seek the help of the Church. Among these seekers will be some so bound by evil spirits they will need deliverance through the name of our Lord Jesus Christ.

The Variety of American Animism

Animism or the worship of evil spirits as practiced in the United States and other Western nations may be classified into four categories.

(1) **Ancient Forms.** Certain ancient forms of
animism such as witchcraft, astrology and Satan
worship have survived underground in so-called
Christian countries. These forms of animism are
practiced in America today.

(2) **Native American Religions.** The religions
of Native American tribes have revived over the
past thirty years and show no sign of dying out.[9]
The animists among Native Americans are actually
a small minority when compared to the number of
Caucasians in America that practice animism in
one form or another.

(3) **Animistic Immigrants.** The influx of ethnic
groups from all over the world has introduced to
the United States several forms of animism such as
voodoo, idolatry, fetishism, fortune-telling and
Eastern mysticism.[10]

(4) **Western Animism.** The fourth category of
animism is Western. Beginning in the nineteenth
century, various spiritualist churches formed.[11] The
movement had its origin in Hydesville, New York,
when the Fox family observed certain noises and
manifestations in the house they had purchased.

The two daughters, Margaret and Kate Fox, developed a way to communicate with the spirit manifestations. Later they attempted to justify their experience with the Bible. This system of Fox-style spiritualism was the supposed communication with the dead. The movement has claimed as many as 20 million followers. It poses as a "church" and has snared many troubled souls with the false hope of communicating with their dead loved ones.

A second form of Western animism is Theosophy. It also emerged in the nineteenth century among sophisticated and well-educated people in New York City. The teachings of Theosophy have been propagated largely by literature and maintained by bookstores in large metropolitan areas which disseminate the teaching among the reading public.[12]

The third variety of Western animism is the popular New Age movement. It is making a greater impact on the culture than any previous westernized animistic religion. Contributing to its success is the current spiritual vacuum in America. The religion of humanism has so pervaded academia, the media, the arts and government as to make the New Age acceptable on the premise that it is an expression of religious pluralism. While the Bible cannot be read in school and students cannot pray in school, there is no government objection to

the use of New Age religious practices in the class-
room. Christians must not be neutral on the New
Age. It must be renounced. Our children need to
be instructed as to its evils.

With this much worship of the powers of darkness prevalent in our country, it is time for the
Church to sound an alarm. The general public, including Christians, are being ensnared by New
Age seminars on miracles and angels. The true
Christian Church believes in miracles and angels
but restricts herself to the Bible in arriving at its
doctrine on these subjects. Psychic phenomena is
not equivalent to the inspired Word of God. The
New Age draws its teaching from Native American spirituality and Eastern religions. Its view of
miracles is non-biblical, formed from animistic
sources.

What scholars now speak of as postmodernism
has created a climate for the renewal of paganism.
Dr. Laurence W. Wood, professor of Systematic
Theology at Asbury Seminary, wrote in the *Asbury
Herald*:

> The biblical condemnation of paganism
> was because it made nature divine. Post-
> modernism at its deepest point is "pa-
> gan" in this sense. You can realize how
> literal post-modernism is because of its

description of demons. You see lots of pictures of demons in post-modern movies, but nothing about a transcendent God. Its demons are aspects of its nature-god. In popular television programs and movies for families, you see grotesque demonic creatures who symbolize our aggressiveness and anxious fears. The post-modern world is a world of hobgoblins, fairies, divination and superstition. One might think that these are not taken seriously in real life, but the rapid growth of the New Age Movement indicates otherwise.[13]

Dr. Wood rightly draws attention to the resurgence of interest in demons in the arts. Not only is it evident in television and Hollywood but in a whole new genre of modern novels devoted to horror. This level of preoccupation with the world of evil spirits has not been around since the Middle Ages. It has already generated and will continue to generate mental health problems. This sick mindset hangs over our country like a plague. It would appear that the sophisticated, high-tech, intellectual Western civilization may produce the lowest and darkest forms of demonic worship in all of human his-

tory. Those of us who take seriously the prophetic Scriptures should not be surprised at this
turn of events. The spirit of Antichrist is at work
in the world. All of this indicates the approach of
the last days. The church or the individual believer that claims to be biblical and evangelical
cannot remain indifferent to this demonic invasion.

The time has come to awaken the Church by a
call to arms. Let us put on the whole armor of God
and be ready to stand in the evil day. That day is
upon us. The Church needs a good offense and a
good defense in this conflict. Christ has mandated
the victory of the Church and has endowed her
with all that is necessary to win.

It is no exaggeration to say that the contemporary Church in America and other Western countries faces her greatest challenge as animism
permeates the culture and seriously competes for
the souls of men. The level of demonic activity in
the West can only be compared to the first century. The apostolic instructions Paul gave the early
Church suddenly are very relevant. In Clinton Arnold's study of Ephesians, he shows the need to
equip believers in the primitive Church for spiritual warfare.

The Epistle to the Ephesians is therefore

> not a response to cosmic speculation. It is
> a response to the felt needs of the com-
> mon people within the churches of west-
> ern Asia Minor, who perceived themselves
> as oppressed by the demonic realm.[14]

Arnold goes on to say that Paul taught that Christians are to depend entirely on Christ in their struggle with the powers of darkness.

Demons concentrate their attacks on the evangelistic outreach of the Church, on the discipleship and maturation of professed believers, on the worship and work of the Church, on her leadership and on the daily lives of God's people. The Church has not been taught to ignore the activity of the enemy but to resist it (1 Peter 5:9). The Church goes on the offense in her resistance of the devil and his attacks. The Christian dare not be passive in this spiritual war. Rather, Paul exhorts the Church to "be strong in the Lord and in the power of His might" (Ephesians 6:10). Our own resources are not sufficient for this battle. We need the whole armor of God with each piece put on by prayer in full obedience to the Lord Jesus Christ.

Paul more than any other New Testament writer presents a theology of the Christian's encounter with the powers of darkness. He thought it necessary for believers to not only be aware of demon activity, but also be able to counter it and live victoriously over these evil powers (Ephesians 6:12-13). The Pauline teaching on this subject was not just theoretical. It was practical for Christians living in the first-century world. These believers lived in communities where the majority of the people were practicing animists. Most Christians were converts from some form of animism. Spiritual warfare with the satanic powers was an integral part of daily Christian living.

As the Church spread in Europe, her influence became so great as to align her with government. So-called Christian nations were formed by this union of Church and State. With the passing of time, the Church in the West began believing that the government and culture had so conformed to Christian ideals that spiritual warfare was no longer urgent. This position was never formally stated, but was clearly demonstrated by the silence of the Church on matters of power encounter.

Over the past seventy-five years, the influence of the Church in the West on government and culture has largely dissipated. Philosophical and sociological shifts in Western countries have resulted in a secular mind-set that either ignores the Church or is antagonistic toward her. There are no countries in the West today where Christianity is the major influence on government and the culture.

The Church is facing something more than unbelief. She is now confronted not only with secularism, but with animism and the malignant powers behind it, often institutionally installed. Consequently, the Church in the West must now witness and work in a context like that of the first-century Church. Pastors and lay people alike must begin to take seriously the teachings of Scripture on our conflict with the powers of darkness.

Added to the decline of Christian influence on society is the massive multiethnic immigration of peoples from all over the world to Western countries. War, poverty, injustice and tyranny have compelled millions to seek refuge in countries like the United States in the hope of finding a better life for themselves and their families. Because many of these immigrants are animists, there is every possibility that in time animism will be the major religious influence in North America. Revival in the Church and the recovery of vital evangelism are two forces able to meet this challenge. Spiritual warfare must be moved from its place of curiosity to a place of practical operation in the life and outreach of the Church.

Much of the description of animism in this chapter comes from firsthand observations while living and ministering among Native Americans. Humanistic secular scholars usually take a different stance when interpreting the observable aspects of these native religions. They use the same data, but come at it from a humanistic mind-set. They even accept the reality of spirits and call it spirituality. But the moral element is absent from their considerations. They conclude that animism is just one more aspect of the human experience.

A good example of this approach to animism among Native Americans is the book entitled *The World of the American Indian* compiled by scholars and published by the National Geographic Society. The editor summarizes the Indian animistic way in these words: "It is a view of the world in balance, of man in harmony with the earth and all things on it. Untold centuries of adaptation to the environment forged the equations."[15] This magnanimous statement seems to be more what the scholars hope is true than what really is the truth. Their humanistic presuppositions rule out an objective look at the reality of Native animism. It is this kind of flawed thinking that blinds North Americans both Native and other from the truth about the real nature of animism.

Obscenity in Animism

Anthropologists have collected thousands of

pages of legends and ceremonies practiced among Native American tribes. The same kind of material has been preserved from animistic peoples all over the world. The Smithsonian Institute contains many volumes of Native American accounts of the worship and behavior of spirits. Obscenity is common in these records. *The World of the American Indian* further reports the activities of certain shamans in the Pueblo tradition:

> Court jester and mediator with the spirit world, the *kossa* invokes supernatural gifts at Tewa ceremonies to protect the pueblo from enemies. In ghostly black-and-white makeup, hair tied in two "horns" with cornshucks, the sacred clowns mask their serious purpose and delight the villagers with pantomime and ribald horseplay. Power to increase fertility in man or beast gives the spirits license to joke obscenely. The ritual dancers pretend they are invisible.[16]

The above quotation is taken from a book prepared by acknowledged scholars. One appreciates the fact that they point out the problem of obscenity in the practices of animistic worship. But to offer a purely humanistic justification for obscenity is not acceptable. The absence of any reference to morality is disappointing.

Because many spirits are designated as unclean, the obscenity in animism should not surprise us. These fallen spirits are wicked and fully given over to the worst forms of immorality. The demons make obscenity a kind of entertainment. By this approach they hope to make their moral garbage acceptable. Obscenity, as introduced by the major networks in this country, is nothing new as they may have thought. It is old stuff. The demons have been doing it for centuries. When obscenity becomes a form of entertainment in a culture, it indicates that demonic powers are getting the upper hand. God condemns obscenity and no amount of rationalism can change the divine fiat. Obscenity has always been and still is the hallmark of paganism.

The cases of demon possession among animists to be discussed in this book will clearly demonstrate the devastating effects of obscenity in animistic religions. It is Christ, the spotless and pure Lamb of God, who stands ready to free those bound by unclean spirits.

Pseudo-spirituality

During the past decade the sciences have become more open to nonphysical reality. Spirituality is now openly discussed among physicians.[17]

While one would ordinarily rejoice at this reversal in attitude by the medical practitioners, there is little reason to rejoice over the present situation. It should be noted that some doctors do understand and value the spiritual dimension of the human personality, but most of them are talking about something entirely different than Christian spirituality. When the scientific or medical community speak of spirituality, they usually mean psychic reality without reference to its source. Their definition is so broad as to take in all forms of psychic experience. It is for this reason that the openness of behavioral science and medicine toward spirituality is not always beneficial.

Professional proponents of this kind of spirituality have also encouraged the bold participation of the occult, Eastern religions and Native animistic reli-gions in the healing process. They apparently are unable to discern the true nature of these spiritual forces. It must be affirmed that there is Christian spirituality and there is non-Christian spirituality. The two are so different that one becomes the antithesis of the other.

True spirituality comes from God alone and is possible only on the ground of faith in Jesus Christ. This spirituality comes as the Holy Spirit applies the grace of Christ and indwells the human personality. The nebulous spirituality of non-Christian re-

ligion is either the product of existential experience
or the activity of the spirit world. The glib talk
about spirituality by the media cannot, in most instances, be taken seriously by believers in the Lord
Jesus Christ.

Pseudo-spirituality disregards morality, truth,
holiness, sin and divine redemption through
Christ. Satan cares little how "religious" humans
become as long as they do not know the truth that
is in Christ. As far as the devil is concerned, one
can weep, dance, laugh, shout, go into trances,
levitate, perform miracles or anything else so long
as that person does not bring his or her sins to the
foot of the cross of Christ, clean up his or her life
and live for God. False spirituality is a major cause
of demon possession in the world.

Academia, the sciences, society and government
often accept religious pluralism as a norm. This
widespread approval has paved the way for the
new definition of spirituality. Historic Christianity
cannot go along with this trend. Christianity's
stand eternally must be "no other gods." Christianity has power, integrity and a message for the
world only when it rests on the truth that the God
of the Bible is exclusively the Creator and the Savior of all mankind. The origin of true spirituality is
in Him alone. There is no light anywhere else. The
Church can only prevail over the current invasion

of strange gods by taking a stand for truth. The Christian community must reach out to a lost world with love while hanging tough on the fact that Christ is the only way.

Endnotes

[1] Levi White, *The Borderland of the Supernatural* (Chicago: The Christian Witness Company, 1905), p. 101.

[2] Ibid., pp. 102-103.

[3] Os Guiness, *The Dust of Death* (Downers Grove: Inter-Varsity Press, 1973), p. 278.

[4] Ibid., p. 281.

[5] Ibid., p. 295.

[6] Coneybeare and Howson, *Life and Epistles of Saint Paul* (New York: George H. Doran, n.d.), p. 258.

[7] David Jeremiah, *Invasion of the Gods* (Dallas, TX: Word Publishing, 1995), p. 14.

[8] Ibid., pp. 22-23.

[9] Duane Champagne, *Native Americans, Portrait of the People* (New York: Invisible Ink Press, 1994), p. 505.

[10] Jeremiah, *Invasion of the Gods,* pp. 27-29.

[11] William B. Williamson, *An Encyclopedia of Religions in the United States* (New York: Crossroads, 1992), p. 310.

[12] Ibid., p. 34.

[13] Lawrence W. Wood, *The Asbury Herald,* fall edition, 1997, p. 6.

[14] Clinton E. Arnold, *Ephesians: Power and Magic* (Grand Rapids, MI: Baker Book House, 1992), p. 171.

[15] *The World of the American Indians* (Washington, DC: The National Geographic Society, 1974), p. 168.

[16] Ibid., p. 168.

[17] Claude A. Fraizer, MD, *Healing: The Finger of God or Scientific Curiosity?* (New York: Thomas Nelson, Inc., 1973), p. 124.

CHAPTER THREE

A Biblical View of Animism

Modern anthropology has made extensive studies of animism in many parts of the world. Although these resources provide valuable information as to the observable aspects of this religious system, only the Old Testament gives an overview of the practices of animism in the ancient world. The New Testament affirms that in Christ every provision for victory has been made.

L ONG BEFORE ANTHROPOLOGY or any other secular disciplines identified and defined animism, the revealed Word of God had done so. Animism as a religion goes back to earth's earliest ages. It is a product of the fall of man.

While it was rampant prior to the flood, more is said about the nature of animism in the early patriarchal period. God called Abraham to leave the animistic culture of Ur of the Chaldees (Joshua 24:2). Abraham's call to follow the true Creator/Redeemer God required his total separation from the corrupt atmosphere of Ur (Genesis 12:1-3). He and his family became pilgrims in a world where the worship of evil spirits was the norm and monotheists were rare.

As Abraham's descendants formed into the nation of Israel and were sent on their way to the promised land, God visited them at Mount

Horeb with full instruction as to how they
should worship so as to be free of any taint of
animism. Among the teachings revealed to
Moses can be found a complete description of the
practices of animism found in the world of that
day. They are identical to the practices of animists in the modern world.

There are some twenty passages in the Old Testament speaking of the evil practices of spirit worship. The most complete treatment of this subject
in the Old Testament is found in Deuteronomy
18:9-14:

> When you come into the land which
> the LORD your God is giving you, you
> shall not learn to follow the abomina-
> tions of those nations. There shall not be
> found among you anyone who makes his
> son or daughter pass through the fire, or
> one who practices witchcraft, or a sooth-
> sayer, or one who interprets omens, or a
> sorcerer, or one who conjures spells, or a
> medium, or a spiritist, or one who calls
> up the dead. For all who do these things
> are an abomination to the LORD, and be-
> cause of these abominations the LORD
> your God drives them out from before
> you. You shall be blameless before the

LORD your God. For these nations which you will dispossess listened to soothsayers and diviners; but as for you, the LORD your God has not appointed such for you.

God spelled out seven forms of spirit worship He condemned. These seven are mentioned in Exodus 7:11 and 22:18, and Leviticus 19:26, 31; 20:6, and are accompanied by the same stern admonitions. God condemns animistic worship and strictly forbids His people to engage in any form of it. It was their practice of animism that compelled the Almighty to judge the Canaanites by extermination. God did not condemn animism because it was an innocent cultural expression of religion. He hated it because of its satanic origin and purpose— to take the place of God. Animism is a system of false gods who are aggressive in their opposition toward God and His people.

A Survey of Hebrew Terms in the Old and New Testament

The Hebrew words used in Deuteronomy 18:9-14 allow some insight into the practices of spirit worship in the ancient world. The best study of these words I was able to find was written at the close of the nineteenth century by

Robert Brown, a biblical scholar in England. A strong evangelical and premillenarian, Brown surveyed the Old and New Testament in his book entitled *Demonology and Witchcraft*, noting every reference to spirit worship.[1]

His careful study of Old Testament Hebrew passages defining the seven forms of animistic practice is especially helpful.

(1) Witchcraft is the English translation of the Hebrew word *ohv*. Of this word Brown said, ". . . it denotes a python or soothsaying demon who evokes the names of the dead by the power of incantation and magical song."[2] This word is frequently translated "familiar spirit" in the Authorized Version.

(2) The second word is *yid-d goh-nee*, translated "soothsayer," which, according to Brown, means "a spirit of divination."

(3) *Gah-nan* means "to act with magic or sorcery." The person who practiced this evil work had a demon that could mesmerize a victim by concentrating on his or her eyes.

(4) The term *kahshaph* has reference to enchantments by means of magic and sorcery.

(5) The next word, *ghehver*, literally means "to bind with magical knots." It is the ability of the demon to bring a victim into bondage.

(6) *Kahsam* was the Hebrew word for divination or

witchcraft. The Greek words used in the Septuagint for *kahsam* means, in one instance at least, "to divine by the flight or the cry of birds." This same practice can be found among modern animists.

(7) The seventh Hebrew term is *nahghash*, which has at its root meaning "to hiss or to whisper." It entailed the use of omens and augury (divination from omens).

Keil and Delitzsch, in their commentary on Deuteronomy 18:9-14, reached the following conclusion:

> Moses grouped together all the words the language contained for the different modes of exploring the future and discovering the will of God, for the purpose of forbidding every description of soothsaying![3]

Israel could not plead ignorance. God had clearly revealed the divine will on this matter. Any contact with the powers of darkness had been strictly forbidden. No religious pluralism can be found in this declaration given by inspiration of the Holy Spirit. The danger of giving in to humanistic religious pluralism cannot be overemphasized. It is a deadly sin in the eyes of God and leads inevitably to judgment. What God taught Israel in

Deuteronomy has not been revoked. With each successive unfolding of divine revelation this truth has been sustained. It is the teaching of the New Testament as well as the Old Testament.

New Testament Demonology

As in the Old Testament there are seven words used in the New Testament to describe the practices of animism.

(1) *Pharmakos*, found only in Revelation 22:15, means "sorcerers." The verse says, "But outside are dogs and sorcerers and sexually immoral and murders and idolaters, and whoever loves and practices a lie." God judges all who are listed here by putting them outside the realm of blessing. They have nothing to look forward to except the agony of an eternal hell.

(2) A closely related Greek work *pharmakeus* is also translated "sorcerer." It is found in Revelation 21:8 which lists those who will be consigned to the second death, the lake of fire. These passages emphasize the enormity of a sorcerer's judgment.

(3) A third Greek word in this family is *pharmakeia* used also in the book of Revelation. John says that though mankind had just been through the awful judgment of the sixth trumpet, it did not repent of its murders nor its sorceries nor its sexual immorality nor its thefts (Revelation 9:21).

(4) Revelation 18:23 uses the same word translated "sorcery," but here it has to do with the wickedness of Babylon, the revelator's allegorical name for the end-time apostate, fallen civilization. This word is taken from *pharmakon* which has as its first meaning "medical drugs." It means the practice of incantations and witchcraft with the use of drugs. As in ancient times, the present-day indulgence in drugs creates a field day for the powers of darkness. With the increase in the drug traffic has come the increase in demon possession in our country.

(5) The word *magos*, translated "sorcerer," is found twice in the thirteenth chapter of Acts. When Paul and Barnabas preached the gospel in Cyprus, a sorcerer named Bar-Jesus resisted their ministry. Paul, through the authority of Christ, caused this sorcerer to be stricken with blindness.

(6) Another famous sorcerer in the New Testament was Simon. The Greek word *mageia* means "one who uses magic to perform sorceries." Acts 8:9 reports that Simon practiced sorceries. The Greek word *mageuo* is the verb form meaning "to practice magic."

(7) The seventh Greek word relating to the works of darkness is found in Acts 16:16. A young girl under the power of a demon was used by her masters as a soothsayer. The word *manteuomai*

means "to divine or foretell." The girl bound by
this spirit was delivered by Paul in the name of
Christ.

It is important to note that these biblical words
for the traffic with evil spirits by human beings are
found in The Acts of the Apostles which is the historical record of the early Church. According to
this record, by the power of Christ the people of
God without exception triumphed over the demon
powers.

In the book of Revelation, the terms show the
renewed intensity of activity when demonic hordes
will be let loose on the earth in unprecedented
numbers during the dark days of the Great Tribulation. All major redemptive events in biblical history have been accompanied by a resurgence of
demonic manifestation. Since Satan was once an
angel, he has extensive knowledge of spiritual
things and always seeks some way to withstand the
unfolding of God's plans. It seems that demon activity even now is beginning to manifest itself with
increasing breadth and intensity in anticipation of
those events.

The New Testament clearly associates idolatry
with witchcraft and other forms of spirit worship.
In the biblical sense, idolatry is a form of animism.
Paul's list of the works of the flesh includes idolatry alongside sorcery (Galatians 5:20). In the first

chapter of Romans (verses 20-23), he explains the origin of idolatry as a firstfruit of the fall of man. With the revelation of God before their eyes, degenerate men chose the image of the corruptible over the incorruptible God who created them. Sinful people, having lost their grip on truth and reason, became easy prey to the deception of Satan and his demons.

A Biblical Definition of Animism

Modern anthropology has made extensive studies of animism in many parts of the world. These resources provide us with valuable information as to the observable aspects of this religious system. But the Bible gives an overview of the practices of animism in the ancient world. Guided by the Holy Spirit, the prophets of Israel put animism in perspective from the divine viewpoint. God spoke by the prophets to warn His covenant people and all who would listen that animism was an abomination in His sight. Those who yielded to the spirit world, God declared, would be brought to judgment.

Jehovah was disturbed with the people of Israel because in the face of clear revelation on the subject they gave themselves shamelessly to the worship of idols indwelt by demons. The full force of God's anger with Israel's idolatry is seen in Hosea

4:17. God told the prophet to say, "Ephraim is joined to idols, let him alone." God gave Ephraim up to the inevitable outcome of the practice of worshiping evil spirits and severe judgment came upon the nation.

God hates idolatry because it is Satan's religion designed by his diabolical mind to counterfeit the real. The heart of Satan's rebellion against God is his desire to be worshiped and recognized as a god. For centuries the devil has created one plan after another to lure the souls of people into spiritual adultery—the worship of the powers of darkness.

The apostle Paul addresses the sin of idolatry in the context of the Lord's Supper. In his first epistle to the Corinthians, Paul devoted part of chapter 10 to the idolaters in Israel, warning them based on the example of Israel's lapse into idolatrous worship. He comes to the point in verses 19 through 22. Idolatry, says Paul, is demon worship. The sacrifices presented to idols are offerings to demons and not to God.

For a Christian there can be no fellowship with demons. Syncretism is not an option. Those who come to the table of the Lord must break all ties with the powers of darkness. God will not tolerate compromise at His table.

The Church in Paul's day had to bear her witness in an animistic culture. The Jews were monotheistic, but all other nations of the known world were animists. In Christ's day, animism had to some degree infected Judaism. The Church was in constant confrontation with the demonic powers behind idolatry. Such a situation once seemed foreign to Christians in the Western world, but now the American Church is beginning to face the same kind of hand-to-hand combat with the powers of darkness as prevailed for believers in the first century. It would be fair to say that we are ill-prepared for such a conflict.

The New Testament Foundations of Spiritual Warfare

The inspired writers of the New Testament took seriously the existence and activity of evil spirits. Demonology was part of the theology of the apostolic Church—not an accommodation to the superstition and ignorance of the day as some scholars have suggested. Rather, the Church's understanding of this phenomenon came from the teachings of Christ and the direct revelation of the Holy Spirit.

Christ always spoke the truth, for it was by the truth, He said, that men would be set free from sin. It is inconceivable that the incarnate Son of God would perpetuate superstition as part of His system of truth. Christ has perfect and complete knowledge of the spirit world and all He said about it was true. Christ considered demons to be spirit personalities devoted to evil and under the direction of Satan. He knew that they sought to possess human personalities for the pleasures and purposes of the powers of darkness. Demons are Satan's servants working to suppress righteousness and godliness. They constitute a well-organized, powerful system that can only be overcome by the power of God.

It is obvious from the four Gospels that Jesus confronted the evil spirits and delivered their victims from demonic possession. Deliverance was an integral part of His ministry and the apostles were firsthand witnesses to both the actions and the teachings of Christ with regard to demons. They learned the ministry of deliverance by precept and example.

The New Testament epistles give evidence that the apostles believed the powers of darkness concentrated on the Church. Their emissaries made war on its meetings, its members and its mission. First-century Christians were taught to discern and withstand the attacks of evil spirits. Spiritual warfare was not a periphery matter.

A pivotal passage on God's provision for spiritual warfare is Colossians 2:13-15:

> And you, being dead in your trepasses
> and the uncircumcision of your flesh, He
> has made alive together with Him, hav-
> ing forgiven you all trespasses, having
> wiped out the handwriting of require-
> ments that was against us, which was
> contrary to us. And He has taken it out
> of the way, having nailed it to the cross.
> Having disarmed principalities and pow-
> ers, He made a public spectacle of them,
> triumphing over them in it.

The Holy Spirit revealed to Paul the place of the atonement of Christ in the immediate and ultimate defeat of Satan and the powers of darkness. According to this passage, Christ experienced direct confrontation with them as He hung on the cross. This explains John's account of the victory of tribulation saints over the demons. They overcame Satan by "the blood of the Lamb" (Revelation 12:11).

According to Scripture, Christ succeeded in stripping the principalities and powers of their strength and authority. The blood atonement is the foundation of spiritual warfare as carried out by the Church. The shed blood of Christ is powerful against the enemy because at the cross Christ crushed the head of Satan according to the promise in Genesis 3:15. The

virgin-born Son of God was the seed of the woman.
He alone could break the power of the evil one. The
blow dealt Satan by the cross took from him his
authority and power. What he does now he does as a
usurper. When Satan is confronted by the victory of
the cross he is powerless.

The believer who undertakes an offensive or defensive position in spiritual warfare must understand
the full extent of Christ's atonement. Any effort to
defeat Satan by mere intellectual or fleshly means
will fail. The power to overcome the evil one is
vested exclusively in the work of the cross.

A Theologian's Definition
of Demon Possession

Charles Hodge, renowned Presbyterian theologian, gave the following definition of demon possession:

> By possession is meant the inhabita-
> tion of an evil spirit in such relationship
> to the body and soul as to exert a con-
> trolling influence, producing violent agi-
> tations and great suffering, both mental
> and corporeal.[4]

Possession differs from other milder forms of demon approach to the human personality in that

the person is under the control of the evil spirit and is helpless against the activity of that spirit. Possession is not a sickness and does not yield to medical treatment. Divine intervention is its only true cure. The indwelling evil spirit must be driven out by a superior power—the Lord Jesus Christ.

Exorcism is practiced among many animistic religions. Such efforts to expel demons cannot be equated with the Christian rite. None of the essential components are present in animistic exorcism—dealing with sin, the affirmation of Jesus Christ, the atonement and resurrection, and faith in the supreme power of God—all characteristics of biblical exorcism. The shaman can only appeal to a demon of a more powerful order to expel a lesser demon. This animistic process lacks the moral and spiritual dimensions of true exorcism.

The Lord Jesus Christ as the incarnate Son of God cast out spirits during His earthly ministry by the power of the Holy Spirit (Acts 10:38; Matthew 12:28). At the cross Jesus faced the entire system of demon powers including Satan himself. He broke their power in our behalf and they are now subject to the authority of Christ (Luke 10:19). The biblical teaching of exorcism maintains that Christ enthroned in glory has delegated His followers to cast out demons in His name (Mark 16:17), which simply means that He allows believers to minister deliverance with His authority. Exorcism is in essence a supernatural act resting on the finished work of Christ and applied by the Holy Spirit. The human instrument is a clean, Spirit-filled believer who with humility and faith claims the delegated authority of Christ to perform the exorcism.

Other Levels of Demon Approach

Having defined demon possession biblically and theologically, it is also necessary to identify other demonic approaches that often become the preliminary steps to full possession. Such inroads are dangerous to the individual's spiritual welfare and should be addressed whenever detected.

Temptation

The universal approach experienced by all Christians is temptation. The experience of the Lord Jesus Christ in the wilderness reveals the evil personality behind temptation (Mark 1:13). Scripture states categorically that God does not tempt anyone (James 1:13). It is always the work of the devil or one of the demons he has dispatched to do the job. They are artists at designing subtle traps to ensnare careless Christians. Temptation is the direct enticement to evil by the powers of darkness.

Oppression

In Peter's message to the Gentiles gathered in the home of Cornelius, the apostle said of Christ that He "went about doing good and healing all who were oppressed by the devil" (Acts 10:38). The same Greek word for "oppress" is used in James 2:6 where the apostle speaks of the tyranny of the rich over the poor, dragging them into court and otherwise making their lives miserable. In the same way, demons harass people with depression, inordinate fear and any other tactic that will produce unhappiness. The oppressed person becomes more and more vulnerable to the enemy's devices, gradually losing control of his or her life. By prayer, instruction and counsel such a person can be freed. This process must be carried out in the power of the Holy Spirit.

Obsession

Another form of demonic approach is obsession. By obsession is meant the believing of a lie proposed by the powers of darkness. One such obsession is the idea that the victim has committed the unpardonable sin. Under this delusion, the person then gives up all hope and lives in utter despair, thinking he or she has forever been cut off from salvation.

Another lie frequently foisted on individuals by

Satan is the notion that an awful calamity is about to overtake them. An endless list of such lies could be compiled. The secret of victory in these cases is found in Second Timothy 2:22-26 where Paul instructs the servants of Christ to correct an individual taken by obsession:

> Flee also youthful lusts; but pursue righteousness, faith, love, peace with those who call on the Lord out of a pure heart. But avoid foolish and ignorant disputes, knowing that they generate strife. And a servant of the Lord must not quarrel but be gentle to all, able to teach, patient, in humility correcting those who are in opposition, if God perhaps will grant them repentance, so that they may know the truth, and that they may come to their senses and escape the snare of the devil, having been taken captive by him to do his will.

Repentance and acknowledgment of the truth set people free from spiritual captivity brought on by believing Satan's lie.

Whatever form the demonic approach may take, there is an antidote in the Word of God. Those ministers and lay people who seek to minister to bound, oppressed and obsessed souls need wisdom in discerning the nature of each person's problem. Do not make the mistake of classifying all demonic problems as possession. Rather, learn all you can about the victim and make a diagnosis based on the facts of the case. The appropriate method for dealing with the victim will be determined by the level of demonic activity evident in that person.

Summary of the Biblical View

Animism is the term used by secular writers in describing the religion of spirit worship. The Bible is not silent on this subject. The origin, practices and effects of animism are all discussed in the Scriptures. God, in the moral law called the Decalogue (Ten Commandments), forbids the worship of spirits or the idols that represent evil spirits. God has spoken: Men and women are not to have any other gods.

Animism according to the inspired Word has its origin in the rebellion and fall of Satan and his angels. The essence of worship of evil spirits is rebellion against God. The many forms of animism in the world have all remained loyal to the evil powers. While some who follow this religion acknowledge a Creator, they worship not Him but evil spirits.

Most forms of animism hold to the pagan idea of an eternal duality of good and evil. The biblical data presents a totally different view of good and evil as they relate to each other. The divine record shows that evil is not eternal. In eternity past it did not exist. The Bible records the beginning of evil in the universe with the rebellion of a created angel now called Satan (Ezekiel 28:11-19; Genesis 3). Evil then became a part of human experience when Satan entered Eden and tempted Adam and Eve to follow him in sin.

The whole thrust of God's redemptive plan is the total defeat of the intelligence behind evil—Satan. It further works to undo the devastating effects of evil on humanity and all creation. Christ came to "destroy the works of the devil" (1 John 3:8). Christ's death and resurrection are the guarantees that evil will come to an end. The kingdom of our Lord Jesus Christ will ultimately conquer every vestige of evil. The devil and his angels, along with all humans who have followed their wicked ways, will be confined forever in the lake of fire (Revelation 20:10-14).

When viewed from the standpoint of revealed truth, evil is temporary, good is eternal. Christianity boldly proclaims the end of evil and the triumph of the kingdom of God. The pagan has only the vain hope that his or her worship and cooperation with the spirit world will give him or her some edge on evil. It is for this reason the animists divide the spirits into good and evil. They hope the good spirits will give them some advantage. They have no idea that the so-called good spirits to which they pray are actually evil. The Bible says that the good spirits—angels—do not accept the worship of men. They worship God alone (Revelation 22:8-9; Hebrews 1:6). From the biblical perspective, all who worship anything or anyone other than God are an abomination to Him (Deuteronomy 18:9-12).

It is the calling of the Church to offer to the animistic people of the world the good news that Christ has defeated the entire realm of evil spirits and can set them free (Mark 16:15-18). But the work of the Church of Jesus Christ as well as the witness and walk of each individual Christian is carried out in alien territory (1 John 5:19). Satan is the god of this world and runs the system in a way that is consistent with his wicked nature. The minute a sinner is saved he or she is postured for a power encounter. Therefore, an important aspect of spiritual development must be training in the reality of spiritual warfare.

Christians should not live in fear of encounters with the powers of darkness, but should be aware of the victory they share with the Lord Jesus Christ "over all the power of the enemy" (Luke 10:19). Through prayer and diligent study of the Word of

God, they learn to detect the enemy and take a stand against his works and ways. While Christians do not face the overt manifestations of demonic power every day such as would be recognizable in a case of demon possession, they are nevertheless dealing with the same malignant spiritual forces.

The intent of these evil powers is to tempt, discourage, confuse and distract the children of God with the hope of reducing their usefulness to the kingdom of God. It is not God's will that we should be victimized by our enemy. In Christ, every provision for victory has been given to the believer. This conflict should not be faced with gloom, fear and despair, but with shouts of victory. Let the high praise of God be in our mouths. Christ has won and He freely shares with His people the spoils of His great victory. The Church does well to face the spiritual conflict with the powers of darkness with a positive and triumphant state of mind. Spiritual warfare is not some kind of spooky sensationalism, but a solemn reality.

The Church must maintain balance in her approach to the doctrine of demonology and its implications for us. A strong biblical foundation will keep it on track in dealing with power encounters and will prevent the fallacy of seeing demonic activity "behind every tree." Distinction must be made between that which is demonic and that which is just human meanness. Care must be taken not to develop an unhealthy preoccupation with the demonic. Satan loves that kind of attention. Keep focused on Christ with all of His purity and glory.

Conclusion

Among my treasured books is a leatherbound copy of the Methodist hymnal published in 1836. An entire section of the hymnal is devoted to hymns on Christian warfare. The Methodist Church at that time was at a high level of revival blessing and its ministers and members had learned the great truth of Christ's overcoming power. One song in this book can be found in most modern hymnals but without all the verses of the original. It is the hymn, "Soldiers of Christ Arise and Put Your Armour On." In the 1836 edition the third verse reads:

> Stand, then, against your foes
>   In close and firm array;
> Legions of wily fiends oppose
>   Throughout the evil day;
> But meet the sons of night,
>   But mock their vain design,
> Arm'd in the arms of heavenly light,
>   Of righteousness divine.

That verse has not been in most hymnals for a long time. Perhaps the modern Church in her love affair with methodology has lost sight of the truth in this verse. The Church has become a hospital for hurting people rather than an army mighty with banners. The teaching of spiritual warfare is of little interest to a Church that looks for her power in the area of technology, communications and Madison-Avenue marketing. This truth will only be of interest to those who feel the stinging blows of the insidious wickedness that characterizes our culture and the fiends of hell who are masterminding the whole affair. The prisoners of war can be set free only by the winning army. It is the stated purpose of God that the Church of our Lord Jesus Christ should be that liberating army.

Endnotes

[1] Robert Brown, *Demonology and Witchcraft* (London: John F. Shaw and Co., 1889), p. 3.

[2] Ibid., p. 14.

[3] C.F. Keil and Franz Delitzsch, *Commentary on the Old Testament,* Vol. 1 (Grand Rapids, MI: Eerdmans, 1980), p. 393.

[4] Charles Hodge, *Systematic Theology,* Vol. 1 (Grand Rapids, MI: Eerdmans, 1952), p. 645.

Deliverance Ministry among Native Americans

Despite a lengthy history of practice and culture rooted in spirit worship, Native Americans are finding freedom from spiritual bondage in Christ. Those who minister to animistic peoples must be able to discern which activities are rooted in darkness. If our sense of spiritual bondage is less than biblical, we will fail in our mission.

PRIOR TO THE coming of Europeans to this continent, all Native American tribes practiced animism. Though the various language groups and cultures had different rituals and approaches to the worship of spirits, their religions were easily identified as animistic. Some tribes believed in a superior God who was the Creator, but their worship was directed to the spirits rather than the Creator.

Still today, their daily lives as animists are controlled by the belief that spirits dwell in everything animate and inanimate. A husband going into the forest to get wood for cooking and heating the family cabin offers tobacco to the spirit that lives in the tree he cuts down for wood. When the nets are drawn, the fisherman leaves an offering to the spirit of the lake or river. At the time of the wild rice harvest, an appropriate offering is given.

In addition to the spirits that indwell natural

objects, the animist must also deal with the spirits of his ancestors. Failure to please these spirits can be disastrous. Among the Chippewas, small spirit houses are built over each grave. At one end of the house is a hole through which the ancestor's spirit may come and go. Just below the hole a tiny platform is built. Relatives bring food, whiskey or anything the deceased liked when he or she was alive. These offerings appease the spirits of their ancestors so they will not place curses on them.

Another feature of Chippewa ancestor worship entails the sacrifice of clothing for the ancestors to wear in the happy hunting ground. Often animists wear old and tattered clothing so they will have the money to present their ancestors with new clothing. In one clan of Chippewas, a worshiper is directed to a special spot in the forest where the recently purchased clothing is placed in a spring in hopes that a great white bear will come from the spirit world and take the clothes to the worshiper's ancestor.

The Grand Medicine Religion

Since ancient times the Chippewa tribes of North America have called their religion the Medewiwin (the Grand Medicine). The tribe's account of the fall of man reveals the origin of their beliefs. After creation, so the story goes, humans and animals lived together in peace. The earth was fruitful, there was no lack of food, and there was no sickness in the earth. Kishemanito, the creator, hung a large vine that reached from heaven to earth. Mankind was sternly warned never to climb this vine, for great calamity would result.

After many years, the legend says, there lived a grandmother who had the responsibility of looking after a very wayward grandson. The grandson would run off just about every day and the grandmother would search for him. One day she thought about the vine. Instead of walking so far to look for the boy, why couldn't she climb up the vine and locate him that way? The old woman knew the prohibition relating to the vine, but reasoned that if she would climb just a little way up it would not matter. Kishemanito would no doubt be too busy to notice her.

One afternoon, when she was especially frustrated and had searched in vain for the boy, she went to the vine and began to climb. Within a short time the sky grew dark and fear came over the people. All of a sudden the vine dropped to the earth and the grandmother was killed. Immediately the people started to experience pain and sickness. Quarrels broke out and peace vanished from the earth. The people were soon weeping and wailing because of their misery. They mourned for an entire night.

When the sun came up the next morning, Kishemanito came down and spoke to the people.

"You have sinned and I have punished you with sickness, sorrow and many troubles," he said. "Now I will cause many beautiful flowers to bloom on earth. I will teach your leaders how to make medicines from the flowers and herbs that will cure your troubles." The legend attributes the powers of the herbs to Kishemanito, but the reality of Chippewa animism is that the medicine men receive their powers from the spirit world.

Take, for example, a Chippewa shaman. He performs his rites by the use of magic and witchcraft. To receive the power for these activities, he enters into a covenant with the spirits, fasting and praying for long periods of time until they take possession of his personality. Shamans, however, appear to be normal persons until they perform the rituals, at which point the spirit takes over. The shaman often includes ancient songs and incantations in his ceremonies, and it is not uncommon to hear the sound of animals coming from his body while he is conjuring.

On one occasion I went to visit a man who lived in a cabin deep in the forest. As I approached the door the sound of a growling bear came from inside. The presence of evil was so strong that I left the area immediately. Later that afternoon I returned to what I had learned was the local medicine man's home. His wife answered the door and invited me in. We talked in generalities for awhile and I asked if I could read a passage of Scripture to them. They consented. But as I began to read I found myself greatly hindered by a powerful resistance in the room. Silently I pled the blood of Jesus and continued.

After finishing the passage, I began to pray. The resistance increased. I opened my eyes for a moment only to see the face of the medicine man twisted and contorted so that he hardly looked human. Again I pled the blood of Christ and continued to pray. By the time I finished, his face had returned to normal. Later I learned that this man was one of the most powerful medicine men in the region. Though in subsequent visits he listened to the gospel, he never turned from the *midewiwin* to Christ.

Those who minister among animistic people are not only contending with superstition but with a deeply entrenched religious system empowered by the forces of evil. The presentation of the gospel of Christ will meet with powerful resistance. The Christian workers dare not be intimidated by such resistance. They must put full trust in the victory of the Lord Jesus Christ over all the powers of darkness. While this particular Chippewa medicine man did not turn to Christ, others did. Some of the most fruitful Native American pastors are converted medicine men.

The Longhouse Religion

The Six Nations or Iroquois of the northeastern United States and southern Ontario, Canada have a unique form of animism. These tribes were among the first to make contact with white settlers and their leaders experienced the awesome results of the invasion of Europeans on this continent.

In the colonial period, a Seneca Indian by the name of Handsome Lake suffered a long illness and during his convalescence had several supernatural spirit visitations. The spirits told him that he was to go to Native Americans with his message. He even claimed that Christ visited him and told him to preach to his own people and that Christ would look after the white man.

The animistic worship he instituted incorporated several ideas from his sketchy knowledge of Christianity. It was, he said, to be carried on in a rectangular building constructed for the purpose of ceremonies and feasts. This meeting place was called the longhouse. The worship began with a cleansing of the worshipers. Each person had a string of shells resembling a rosary which they ran through their hands as they confessed their sins.

The Longhouse religion was cleverly designed to discourage Native Americans from accepting the gospel being preached among them. It has survived to the present day among the Six Nations tribes. The account that follows concerns an individual from the Seneca tribe, which is part of the Six Nations.

A young Seneca woman I shall call "Lorna," the daughter of a powerful Longhouse shaman, professed faith in Christ at a Baptist mission on the Seneca reservation in New York state. Shortly after, Lorna learned of the Mokahum Indian Bible School in Minnesota and was encouraged by the local missionaries to attend.

The next fall, she arrived at the school to prepare to become a Christian worker. A pleasant person and well-liked by students and faculty, Lorna appeared quite normal except for her inability to speak when she wanted to testify. She encountered the same difficulty in prayer. The words simply would not come. We assumed that perhaps shyness or a speech impediment accounted for this behavior.

One day, a few weeks into the semester, the dean of women went to Lorna's room to discover why she was not in class. The dean found her in a coma. She was taken to the U.S. government Indian Hospital where she remained for twelve days under medical care. At that point, the doctor in charge summoned me to his office to discuss her case. He was very puzzled. With all of their medical tests and psychiatric consultations, the staff could find no basis for the symptoms Lorna displayed. The doctor said that they were baffled, but with no reason to detain her any longer they were going to release her to us.

"Reverend," he said, "we can do nothing for her. Perhaps you can."

Meanwhile, on the campus, students and faculty had been waiting on God in earnest prayer. There was a consensus among the faculty that we were dealing with demonic powers. We brought Lorna back to the school determined to seek God and search His Word until she was released from whatever power possessed her. That day was the beginning of an eight-month journey that would have far-reaching implications for the work of the gospel among Native Americans.

Once Lorna was settled in her room, the students and faculty gathered for prayer while several of us went to visit her. As we began to pray, she fell into a coma. I was impressed to try the spirit according to First John 4:1-2. None of us in the room had ever done anything like this, so we were cautious. I finally got up enough nerve to say, "Has Jesus Christ come in the flesh?"

Almost instantly a voice, not her own, answered, "No."

All doubt as to what we were dealing with vanished.

With my Bible open to Mark's Gospel, I said to the demon, "In the name of Jesus Christ I command you to come out of her and leave."

At that point, she went into a violent convulsion followed by a piercing cry as the demon departed. (In searching the Scriptures, we could not find any instruction as to where to send them. We therefore followed the practice of commanding the spirit to go and never to return.) The evil spirit hit the wall in her room and every other wall as it passed through the building and on up the hill through two other buildings. The young lady sat up perfectly normal and talked with us. And, as you can imagine, the people in those other buildings came to see what had happened.

Over the next several hours we had a crash course in power encounter. But when the prayer meeting was resumed, she once again went into a coma. Some of us noticed that in the book of Mark Jesus commanded the demons to give their names prior to being cast out (5:9). We decided to use that procedure. When we asked the name of the demon, it hesitated, but soon responded with a name. We then commanded it to leave. It did so, but another promptly manifested itself. The same process was repeated several times, always with the same results.

Someone noted that in the case of the demoniac of the Gadarenes Jesus asked for its name which was "Legion." The purpose of this question was to establish the fact of multiple possession. By this time we were wondering how extensive her possession was. Following the pattern of Christ, the question was asked and the demon admitted its name was Legion. It took much prayer before it departed.

After Legion left, a large group of demons left one after the other. These spirits were all associated with the Longhouse religion. Several times during the long period of her deliverance, the name Legion would surface and a cluster of related demons would be expelled. (The most powerful and violent demons were those associated with the name Legion.) In every such incident there was a struggle requiring hours of prayer and counsel to learn more about the victim's involvement with sin or animistic worship that provided the ground of possession. It was helpful to take the victim through a renunciation of the ground she had thus given the enemy.

Over a period of days, time was given to learning more about Lorna's background. She was born and raised in an animistic home, her father being a "false face" dancer who participated in the healing rituals of medicine men. His daughter was sickly as a child and had been doctored by their traditional methods. She recalled that a strange power came over her the first time she was exposed to the false face ritual. According to her testimony, she rolled like a ball all over the room and had no control over her actions. Repeated efforts to heal her only intensified her problem.

As she grew older, she was placed in a Catholic school. Strange symptoms and behavioral problems continued to plague her life. At one point, the decision was made to seek medical help for her, but no chemical or physical basis was found for her symptoms. After psychiatric evaluation, she was placed in a state mental institution, but since she was not harmful to others or herself, she was released and returned to her home reservation.

There was a parallel between the classification of demons cast out and the various stages of her life. Having become possessed as a child, each new exposure to evil made her even more vulnerable, resulting in a very complex multiple possession. Records were kept of the names of the evil spirits cast out of her. In excess of 300 spoke audibly and gave their names. The spirits often resisted the command to reveal their names, for the giving of their names consistently disclosed the cause of the possession, thus blowing their cover and allowing easy expulsion.

A study of the names of demons in a victim of animism shows a marked contrast with those usually encountered in cases from Western culture. Some names are the same, but most are vastly different. This young Seneca lady, while reared in animistic culture, had been exposed to typical Western culture. She had a demon of "bingo" and "slot machines." We learned that she was addicted to both of these practices. Another strong demon called "filthy magazines" tormented her until she confessed her sin and the demon was exorcized.

The more common names were pride, adultery, suicide, fear, lust and anger. Lorna was also afflicted with spirits of lying, deceit, stealing, jealousy, swearing and mockery.

Medical doctors had been puzzled by the symptoms of illness for which they could find no cause. Early in the process of exorcism, a demon of sickness was exposed. A demon of St. Vitus dance and of tuberculosis were later cast out. One demon identified itself as "obstruction in the lower bowel" and another gave its name as "gallbladder." She displayed the symptoms of all of these illnesses.

While one would have to reject on scriptural grounds the notion that every sickness has a demon behind it, it might be seen from this case that evil spirits can inflict sickness in some circumstances. Lorna's health improved remarkably as the deliverance progressed.

A very interesting category of spirits targeted her new-found faith. A demon of unbelief sought to create doubt. One gave its name as "hindrances to prayer." Every time she sought to pray, her flow of thought would be lost and she could not finish. After the expelling of that demon, she prayed with great fluency and understanding. A spirit called "hindrances to spiritual life" also resided in Lorna. It was the conclusion of all who knew her case and had opportunity to deal with it that she was a Christian. She made great effort to serve God and had great sorrow over her failures. When she professed Christ and was baptized no one sensed her condition. The missionaries later told us they had had no experience with deliverance.

Lorna's arrival at Mokahum Indian Bible School thrust her into an atmosphere of prayer and intense spiritual activity. As a new student, she was required to take a course on Christology. It was a simple course covering every passage in the Old and New Testaments relating to Christ. She seemed unable to comprehend the material. At times she appeared troubled. She could not speak when asked a question. Later we learned that the demonic powers would so take over that she could not see the blackboard nor hear a word of the lecture.

The combination of prayer, Bible study and sincere worship also greatly agitated the spirits resident in her personality. As the deliverance process continued, prayer meetings were held around the clock. Fasting was also an important factor in this ministry. We waited on God for wisdom and discernment to get through each day, but language and culture presented unique problems. Even the demons would speak in Seneca! The victim was a Seneca and no one else on campus spoke or understood her language and none of us were knowledgeable in the ideas and practices of the Longhouse religion in which she had been reared. The Lord undertook in remarkable ways to help us with this problem.

At first we wrote down the words phonetically with the idea of sending them to her home reservation for translation. But one of the Chippewa pastors noted that when he spoke in Chippewa the demons understood him. He then commanded in the name of the Lord Jesus Christ that the demons translate what they had said. Immediately they responded to this command and spoke in English. Later, when visitors from her tribe arrived on campus, they checked the translations and found them to be correct. The same Indian pastor was given discernment and had the ability to name demons and readily cast them out.

One day, as the deliverance team began to pray in preparation for another session, a very strong spirit manifested itself by producing all kinds of physical contortions in Lorna's body. He gave the name "Third Demon of Handsome Lake." This spirit was apparently the leader of the group.

After hours of prayer and commanding, a total of five Handsome Lake demons were exorcized. One of this group said that he was a false Christ. Almost immediately another group related to Handsome Lake surfaced. The first was called "Handsome Lake False God," the next had the name "Moccasin God." During the next few sessions all the spirits cast out were related to Longhouse ceremonies and healing rituals. These spirits were very demonstrative. One called "Longhouse Drum Dance" caused her body to levitate and dance. It should be noted that the victim was in a coma and had no awareness of this activity. This was followed by the corn dance and the strawberry dance and the corn soup dance. Many other dances and rattles were mentioned as names of the spirits.

Every occasion on which Lorna was subjected to healing ceremonies was significant in her possession. This was confirmed when certain demons identified themselves as coming from certain medicine men, including her father. Names of the medicine men were given by the demons as they were cast out. We had opportunity to verify that all five of these were actual practicing medicine men on her reservation.

While this group of demons was being expelled, a demon emerged calling himself "Chief Cornplanter." Cornplanter was a prominent Six Nation chief and supporter of Handsome Lake. In the system of animism, powerful shamans send demons on people to torment them and hinder them. It was apparent that the spirit world was alarmed that one so completely under its power would call upon Christ for deliverance and salvation. A battle line had been drawn. In the months that followed we were to learn just how far-reaching this spiritual battle was.

Some weeks into the deliverance process a legion of spirits was expelled. The ten leaders of this legion used the name "Chief Servant of Lucifer" followed by an explanation of their work. The first was called "Chief Servant of Lucifer to hinder Alliance work among the Native Americans." Another was to hinder the gospel ministry among the Six Nations. The names of others revealed their job descriptions of causing sickness, hindering the study of God's Word, causing people to backslide and resisting prayer. As these demons were cast out, Lorna experienced a remarkable release. From that time on she was able to easily memorize Scripture and pray with noticeable freedom. It became obvious that she had a good mind and that her former symptoms were not the result of inferior intellectual powers but were the direct result of demonic possession. At this point she became very cooperative and had an intense desire to be fully delivered.

A demon named "Indian Tobacco" was very strong and when it manifested a strong scent of tobacco filled the room. (A small native tobacco plant is used by many Indian tribes in their ceremonies and rituals.) Closely related to the tobacco spirit was a group of five demons that bore the name "Pighead Dance." Lorna's face became distorted to look like a pig and the room was filled with the odor of pigs. It was so strong at one point that we had to leave the room. Someone suggested we command the odor to stop. When this was done in the name of Christ, the odor was gone. Evidently this was a tactic by the enemy to confuse and distract the members of the deliverance team. We gradually learned that violence and dramatic demonstrations were part of the enemy's strategy to hinder Lorna's deliverance.

Just as the Christian worker has the authority to cast out demons in the name of Christ, he also has

the authority to restrict the activity of the demons.
Jesus said, "Behold, I give you the authority to
trample on serpents and scorpions, and over all the
power of the enemy, and nothing shall by any
means hurt you" (Luke 10:19). When we learned
this truth, we were better able to cope with the
manifestations induced by the demons.

The Demonic Invasion of Culture

As the days went by we became more and more
aware of how deeply the animistic religion of the
Longhouse people penetrated their culture. Many
of the dances and ceremonies were not just innocent cultural activities. The spirits cast out gave
the names of a whole series of dances common
among the Six Nations such as "Green Corn
Dance," "Strawberry Dance," "Dance in the Dark"
and others. Each of these dances had sacred meaning in their religion and were not just social occasions. The demons also gave names relating to
sacred articles such as drums, rattles, feathers,
beads, wood ashes, bow arrows, Indian costumes,
cornhusk masks and turtle rattles. Lorna apparently was invaded by these demons while attending the dances.

Several weeks into the process, exorcism became
difficult. Time was taken to counsel with the victim to see if there might be an area in which she

was holding back. With a negative response to that question, a prolonged season of prayer was called to seek the face of God for enlightenment. We were alternately praying and searching the Scriptures for understanding when our attention was called to Acts 19:19-20:

> Also, many of those who had practiced magic brought their books together and burned them in the sight of all. And they counted up the value of them, and it to-taled fifty thousand pieces of silver. So the word of the Lord grew mightily and prevailed.

The new converts at Ephesus were coming out of paganism and realized they had to make a complete break with all their magic and witchcraft paraphenalia. These items were gathered in great number and burned.

After brief reflection on this passage, I was reminded of some items which had been given to me by new believers. A converted medicine man from the Assinaboine tribe had given me a rattle he had used in the worship of the sun. Also hanging on my office wall was a large flat drum that had been used in *medewiwin* ceremonies. We decided to collect and burn these items.

As we started to collect them, the drum started to beat of its own accord and the rattle began shaking violently. Had I been alone in the room, I would have doubted what I saw, but there were a dozen or more people with me. Immediately we cried out in prayer and the manifestation stopped. Then a command was given in the name of Jesus Christ for the demons to leave these objects. We then proceeded to the yard and burned them.

This event opened the eyes of missionaries and Native Americans alike to the seriousness of this kind of power encounter. For some weeks prior to this incident I had found it difficult to think or study in my office. After the burning, the deliverance ministry took on new effectiveness. There was also a greater freedom in the atmosphere on campus.

Other items were located and burned. The missionaries and Native American leaders discussed this problem and concluded that Christians should be careful in collecting artifacts that may have been used in spirit worship and may have resident powers. (Ouija boards, often used in demonic activity, are a case in point.) Missionaries should also take special care in selecting curios for display purposes.

We learned from this experience the wisdom of consulting mature Native American believers to learn how to discern between those things which are merely cultural and those which are rooted in spirit worship. Many animistic rituals are used to make contact with the spirits—singing, drumming, use of the sweat lodge, the burning of cedar boughs, sweet grass and tobacco, to name a few.

To have power in the ministry of deliverance, one must separate from all such ceremonies, rituals and objects that have been dedicated to the powers of darkness. Too often these things are dismissed as superstitions. The truth is that they are part of a dark and sinister reality.

There is no place for compromise with the works of darkness. Those who minister to animistic people must be able to discern those activities which are rooted in spirit worship. Such discernment is vital in spiritual warfare. If we are sent to loose the bound, we must understand what it is that binds them. If our sense of spiritual bondage is less than biblical, we will fail in our mission.

CHAPTER FIVE

The Powerful Effects of Revival

Today, as the evangelical Church faces the task of evangelizing the great diversity of animistic people now residing in America, there will undoubtedly be many cases of deliverance. Controlling demonic forces must be challenged before the harvest can be gathered in. Deliverance is sometimes a significant dimension of evangelism.

WITHIN DAYS OF the onset of Lorna's battle, all of our faculty began to realize that her condition was only part of the battle that engaged us. This war had much broader dimensions than the help of one individual. Native American Christians advised us that the Chippewa medicine men in the Leech Lake Reservation and some other reservations had learned of this case and were publicly announcing that they would kill Lorna. Prayer was increased and precautions were taken to protect her. A registered nurse volunteered to stay with her and guards were placed at the doors at night.

But our precautions, it soon became apparent, were of no avail. Each morning the nurse found Lorna covered with black and blue welts. After intense prayer, the welts would go away. The next few days were a pitched battle with the powers of darkness as we laid hold of God on the grounds of

Christ's shed blood and asked that the spirits in-
flicting these wounds be bound and the medicine
men responsible be bound from further activity.
God heard these prayers. That phase of the war
ended.

Meanwhile, revival broke out among the Native
American Christians in the immediate community.
The Bible school chapel was filled to capacity every
night with attendees from an eighty-mile radius.
Both Caucasian and Native American people were
touched as a wave of deep conviction of sin came
over the community. It didn't matter who
preached—the results were the same. The altar
would fill the moment the invitation was given. At
some services, people began going to the altar even
before the message was finished. Persons long resistant to the gospel melted under the conviction
of the Spirit. As soon as the seekers found peace
they returned to their seats, and the altar would
again fill with people. This pattern repeated itself
for several hours without a break.

Services were never less than four hours long
and often continued until daybreak. None of us
who was present can ever forget the overwhelming
sense of the presence of God that characterized
those meetings. The singing was so uplifting. "Oh,
for a Thousand Tongues" was sung at almost every
service. Songs on the blood of Christ were repeated

again and again. On one occasion the congregation sang acapella for two full hours without a break, passing naturally from one hymn to the next. Streams of heavenly joy flooded the sanctuary.

Those who led in prayer were extraordinarily exercised in spirit. Prayer meetings were in session around the clock. Many fasted and prayed. A tremendous spiritual breakthrough was experienced by a number of the Native American believers and churches in the area. When this case of deliverance first began, many were paralyzed with fear. But as they witnessed the power of the Lord Jesus Christ over the demons, they too were set free from fear.

Among those attending the meetings was an elderly Chippewa man who had accepted Christ a year earlier. He had up to this time refused to be baptized. On seeing the power of Christ to cast out demons, he asked for baptism. He said, "I have worshiped evil spirits for seventy years and I know how powerful they are. But now I know that the Lord Jesus Christ is much more powerful."

He was baptized in his village, a stronghold of the Grand Medicine, and all the medicine men of that area came to observe the ceremony. He knew full well that to be baptized as a Christian would forever cut him off from the Grand Medicine. He had been a fourth degree *manido*, a powerful shaman in his own right. Standing in the water just offshore from the *medewigan*, the center of Grand Medicine worship, before his friends, family and the leaders of his old religion, he told of his personal experience of salvation and testified to the wonderful grace of Christ and of His supreme power. This was one of the overflow blessings from the revival at the Bible school.

Up to the time of this baptism, the years of missionary labor had produced only three believers in the village. After Wabishkwanikwud's baptism, the chapel was filled every Sunday. Souls came to Christ in significant numbers. There was never another Grand Medicine ceremony in the village of Squaw Point. The power of the Lord Jesus Christ had triumphed over the powers of darkness.

Similar movings of the Spirit occurred in other villages such as Onigum which had only a small group of believers. They came to the Bible school and were deeply touched by the revival. A few weeks later they had the opportunity to glorify the Lord in an unusual circumstance. A well-known medicine man who was famous for his ability to locate lost things lived in their village. Often in the winter when the lakes were frozen, people would walk on soft ice and fall into the water. If they were alone, they would soon die from hypothermia.

A drunkard in the village of Onigum had fallen through the ice some months before. As was often the practice, the United States rangers, when attempting to recover the body, would seek the services of this medicine man. The small group of revived Christians decided this was the time for their community to see the power of Christ. Upon learning that on a certain day the medicine man was to conjure in order to locate the missing body, the Christians called a prayer meeting. Their request was simple: "Lord, wherever the medicine man says the body is located, move it to the opposite side of the lake." God heard their prayer and the body was found at the opposite side of the lake from the medicine man's directions. The rangers never again used the medicine man to locate bodies and the answer to prayer had a powerful effect on the people of that village.

The moving of the Spirit at the Bible school continued for ten weeks, but the overflow was to continue for years to come. A major battle had been won over the resistance of the animists in that area. For fifty miles around the school the Grand Medicine shamans stopped holding their ceremonies, making it easier to preach the gospel in the villages. Above all, the revival produced some significant Native American Church leadership. Some of the young men became key evangelists and pastors in the years that followed and experienced revival in their own ministries.

Another effect of the revival was that a host of people were enlightened as to the nature of spiritual warfare. Until the revival, most of the missionaries and Native people had no firsthand experience with power encounters. They had sensed the oppressive darkness that prevailed in so many villages, but had not claimed the victory of Christ over those evil powers. All of us were changed by this demonstration of the authority and power of Christ over the demon forces.

The teachings of Paul on Christian warfare became real. Our prayer life was radically altered. We learned that spiritual warfare was more than the exorcism of demons. It entailed worship, intercession, holy living and Spirit-endued ministry. John Bunyan's *Pilgrim's Progress* seemed very realistic after eight months of battling for Lorna's deliverance from over 300 demons that possessed her.

Victory at Last

While the revival was in progress, the deliverance team continued to meet in long sessions with the victim to complete the work of freeing her from the bondage of the enemy. The case often took interesting turns. At one stage the problem of fear seemed to grip everyone on campus. At the same time, the children of the ministry team were being plagued with sickness and the atmosphere at the school seemed heavy.

When the situation was at its worst, I received a telephone call that the Indian agent for the reservation wanted to introduce me to a man who was visiting him. I sent word for them to come, but in my heart I was not enthused about the interruption in my schedule. Little did I know that the man the agent was bringing to my office was the Rev. John Carlson, veteran Lutheran missionary to Bolivia, South America. I was reluctant to tell them of our battles, but the impression kept returning to me to do so.

After I gave them a brief update on our ongoing confrontation with the enemy, to my utter amazement Rev. Carlson began telling of his experience with casting out demons in Bolivia. The discussion continued for the remainder of the morning and I learned some very important truths that eventually turned the tide in Lorna's deliverance.

In response to the problem of excessive fear and multiple cases of sickness among us, Rev. Carlson suggested that we pray in each building on the campus and command all evil spirits to leave in the name of the Lord Jesus Christ. Carlson explained that demons were lingering on the campus and reinforcements had come to harass us and hinder the progress being made in the case.

Immediately after the agent and Rev. Carlson left, I called together the faculty and staff to share with them what I had learned. We also invited some of the more mature students to join us in an extended time of prayer. We went to each building, repeating the prayer and commanding the demons to leave. By the time we were done, we could sense the difference in the atmosphere. The attacks of sickness and the waves of fear stopped. We had learned a new secret of spiritual warfare.

Roman Catholic Influence

One day a demon gave its name as "The Rosary." This came as a surprise since we were not aware at that time that Lorna had had any association with Catholicism. We learned that for a period of months she had been placed in a Roman Catholic institution. To her animistic beliefs in the gods of the Longhouse, she added the ritual symbols of the Roman Church, including offering worship to the statues which she viewed as gods.

Apparently a group of spirits entered her at that time. The most unusual was a demon that gave its name as the "Idol of Jesus." Three other spirits gave the names "Idol of Mary," "Idol of Joseph" and "Idol of the Catechism."

Other Native Americans brought into Catholicism without a conversion or real knowledge of the

Christian faith fell into the same kind of idolatry. It was not uncommon to find both the crucifix and a fetish hanging over the head of the sick. We were to encounter this category of evil spirits in other cases of possession among animists.

Impact of Western Culture

The demons that entered Lorna initially were related to the animistic practices of the Longhouse. But as time went by, many other kinds of spirits entered her personality, bringing her deeper and deeper into bondage. Some spirits attacked the body while others concentrated on her mind. Still others came by way of the bad habits she developed because of her degenerate spiritual condition. Gambling, drinking, drugs and many other vices became part of her life. All of these had to do with non-Indian culture. Her experiences with the dark side of the white man's world only intensified her inner anguish.

Today, as the evangelical Church faces the task of evangelizing the great diversity of animistic people now residing in America, there will undoubtedly be many cases of deliverance. The condition of these people will only be worsened by the adverse effects of the open sin in our culture, including demonic undercurrents in certain American music and art forms. My observation is that about forty years ago the first cases of persons demonized by certain kinds of popular music emerged. That has only intensified across the intervening years. It is now widely recognized that the occult has invaded the extreme music styles which mesmerize America. The powers of darkness have no qualms about inserting themselves into any human activity that is opened to them.

Extraordinary Strength

One fall, a Chippewa girl arrived at the Bible school. According to the missionary, she had professed Christ as her Savior and showed evidence of conversion. She had a good voice and often played the guitar and sang in chapel services or on team assignments. Most people who heard her sing commented on the unusual voice quality and style, but many began to feel uncomfortable when she sang.

About three months into the semester, the dean of women noticed the girl's absence from class and went to the dormitory to check on her. She found her in a coma. (There were several incidents of students being found in a comatose state.) The deliverance team immediately went to prayer. We did not know then that this would be the most violent case of possession we had encountered.

This young lady was small, but under demon power showed extraordinary physical strength. On one occasion she got out of bed, rolled under it, picked it up and began to pound the walls with it. On this occasion there were seven strong men present for security purposes. Since she was tearing the room apart, the men attempted to restrain her. Suddenly she rose to her feet and knocked all seven to the floor. A new lesson was learned during this episode—ordinary physical strength is no match for demons.

I was one of those men. As I got to my feet, the Lord prompted me to command her in the name of the Lord Jesus Christ to stop this behavior. She froze on the spot and could not move. I then commanded her to return to her room and be quiet. From that point on there was no further violence. In subsequent cases we often used this commanding procedure when violence threatened.

This Chippewa girl had been raised as an animist and had shown interest in the gospel for only a short time. Many of the evil spirits cast out of her were from the Grand Medicine tradition. She showed a fascination with music both Native American and Western. A whole cluster of demons gave the names of popular singers. At the sound of their voices on the radio or via recording she would go into a trance.

Hers was one of the few cases where deliverance failed. She began to show great resentment toward the deliverance team and would not cooperate with them. No amount of spiritual counseling seemed to affect her. She finally categorically stated that she did not want to give up the spirits that possessed her. The missionary from her reservation came and attempted to persuade her to stay, but she would not yield. She had made a choice and would have to live with the consequences.

The missionary drove her to her father's home on the reservation. A practicing medicine man deeply committed to animism, he was happy that she was returning but had no idea of what was about to happen. As she got out of the car, the demons took over. She went for her father, picked him up and threw him through the door, almost killing him. His injuries laid him up for months. This girl weighed about 110 pounds and her father weighed over 200 pounds. This display of demonic strength put fear into the whole community. When she came out of the manifestation, she too was horrified at her father's condition. Unwilling to seek the help of the gospel, she propelled herself into the worst kind of sin and darkness. Down a spiral of agony and torment comparable to Dante's *Inferno*, she plunged to an early grave.

There are two important lessons to learn from this account: (1) The authority of Christ can subjugate the strongest demon; and (2) if the victim willfully refuses the help of Christ and His servants, no effort of exorcism will succeed.

Animism among the Assiniboines

An Assiniboine Native American family came to the Bible school. After a few days in an atmosphere of prayer and Bible study, the husband became very troubled. He asked for prayer that he would be free of the spiritual forces that were bothering him. A group of students and faculty members gathered at his cabin to pray with him. Soon after the prayer session began, the man went into a coma. Assuming it was the work of an evil spirit, the leader asked the spirit if Jesus Christ had come in the flesh. A strange voice answered in the negative.

This was the beginning of several weeks of deliverance ministry. The victim went by the English name of Charlie. He had been deeply involved in the Sundance tradition. Prior to the dance, the dancers fast for four days, leaving them in a weakened condition. Leather thongs are then fastened through the skin of their chests by means of wooden pegs and the men make their way to a circular brush arbor. A center pole supports the roof. With the other end of the leather thongs tied to the pole, the dancers place themselves around the outside wall. As the drums begin and the singers start their chant, the dancers commence their frenzied gyrations. Their goal is to dance from sunup to sundown. The physical ordeal of this dance is intensified by the pulling of the leather thongs on the flesh of the dancers.

After an hour or two of such physical exertion, the dancers sometimes collapse. The medicine man then strikes the center pole with a wild turkey bone whistle and a stream of what appears to be water spurts out, landing on one of the dancers. He instantly springs to his feet and begins to dance with unusual energy. Having been present at a Sundance, I can verify the intense and oppressive demon presence that surrounds the place. Charlie's experience in the Sundance was the basis of his possession.

Charlie had also spent time in the sweat lodge performing rituals and learning the secrets of the medicine man. The spirits that entered him through these animistic rites opened him to such sins as gambling, immorality and drinking. The group of demons which brought him into bondage to these sinful practices were gradually depleting his physical strength and resources. In great distress, he finally found help through the faithful efforts of a local missionary and Charlie and his family made a profession of faith in Christ. They heard of the Indian Bible School and decided to come for training.

Once, while we were praying with Charlie, his mouth opened and two demons began to argue as to which would leave first. This was one of only two occasions where we heard spirits conversing with each other. The Scriptures speak of organization and hierarchy in the spirit world where certain principalities and powers maintain and exhibit authority over lesser powers. In Charlie's case, there seemed to be a pecking order. The most powerful of the two spirits soon prevailed and the other left. After a lengthy struggle of prayer and commanding, the second spirit left.

There was also a spirit called "Wild Turkey Bone Whistle" and another from the sweat lodge. There was a demon of rattles and a demon of sweet grass which was used for incense in animistic ceremonies. There were also whispering and muttering spirits. According to Isaiah 8:19, these are demons that imitate the dead. Ancestor worship is common in animistic religions, including that of traditional Native Americans.

Before Charlie's deliverance was complete, his teenaged daughter was found in a coma in her dormitory room. Obviously vulnerable to the spirits and growing up in an atmosphere of spirit worship, she too had been possessed. Like many other Indian young people she had experienced the worst side of Western culture. Her case was a combination of animistic spirits and demons of wicked behavior.

Some very powerful medicine men were in charge on the Fort Belknap Reservation, the home of Charlie and his family. While ministering one summer in that area, I felt constrained to visit the older people and give them the gospel. Since I did not know the local language, the Lord provided an excellent interpreter, Mr. Black Hoop.

One afternoon, the interpreter and I came to a cabin occupied by two of the most powerful medicine men in the area. They welcomed us and after some palaver I began unfolding the gospel. Beginning in Genesis, I carefully traced the plan of redemption to show that Christ was not the white man's God, but that He was the Savior of the world. After about an hour, one of the medicine men, Sam King, interrupted me, saying he had an appointment. He invited me to return the next day and finish the story. He told us that over fifty years earlier a man had told him the same story. He had been waiting all these years to hear it again.

The next morning Mr. Black Hoop and I arrived at Sam's cabin. It took another three hours to go through the whole plan of God to save humanity through Christ. I then asked Sam if he was interested in accepting the Lord Jesus Christ, the Son of God, to be his Savior. Through the interpreter he told me that he wanted Christ to come into his heart. I prayed, then asked him to pray. This was rather difficult since our conversation had to be interpreted. But we left that cabin with the strong conviction that old Sam King had been saved.

It was not until the next spring that we had verification of his conversion. The first thing I did when I arrived at the reservation was to inquire about him. They said he had passed away only a few weeks before my coming. As death drew near, Sam called the old medicine men, the leaders of the Sundance, around his bed. He asked if the white man who told him this story of Jesus could tell him the story once again. They answered that I was many miles away and could not come. He then replied that he was sorry, for he would like to hear it one more time.

Speaking to his fellow shamans, Sam told them that he had found peace in his heart since Christ had saved him. He died with a smile on his face. The Sundance leaders looked at each other in amazement. They said, "We have watched many men die, but have never before seen a man die smiling." They concluded that this must be the true religion. The end result of Sam King's conversion was the establishment of a church in that area.

The significance of his experience should not be overlooked. He was a shaman and had been in spirit worship all of his life. One must ask how he was set free from the evil spirits without, as far as we know, the process of exorcism. I do not have the answer. But I do know that each of these men was very intelligent and understood the issue of Christ's Lordship. When they accepted Christ they knew that in doing so they must break with the evil spirits they formerly served.

Other Shamans Converted

A Seneca man about sixty years of age was saved and immediately set free from all demon power. He was a false face dancer in the medicine ritual of the Longhouse. It was his practice to communicate with the spirits and he depended on them for his power. Returning home the night he found Christ, it seemed that the hordes of hell were surrounding his house. He stood in the center of the kitchen floor and in a loud and clear voice testified to the spirits: "I have taken Jesus Christ as my Lord and Savior. I will not serve you any more. I want nothing to do with you evil spirits. Go in the name of Jesus and never return." From that day on he lived a godly and fruitful life as a Christian.

Pete Grey Eyes, a Navajo medicine man, found Christ at a Navajo Mountain church. According to Herman Williams, the pastor at the time, Pete was being challenged by another powerful medicine man. He knew there was the possibility that the conflict would end in his death. He also knew about the church, but he was so devoted to the traditional ways that he avoided Christianity altogether. In this threatening situation, however, one night Pete took his family to church. After hearing the gospel, he took Christ as his Savior.

Pete and his family went home to find the powers of darkness occupying his property. Owls came along with animals of various kinds. (In the native tradition the spirits sometimes work through animals.) He sensed the demons were going to try to hold him back from following Christ, so he walked out in the yard and spoke to the spirits. After listing everything he owned, Pete said, "All of these things belong to the Lord Jesus Christ. There is nothing here for you. You must all go. Goodbye." The owls left and the animals left, and the presence of the evil spirits was gone. They did not return.

Pete Grey Eyes has served for years as a respected church elder. He is very gifted at exorcism and has been used of God in his tribe to free many from the powers of darkness. The church has constructed a native *hogan* near the church building where the elders, Bible women and other mature believers pray for the demon possessed and cast out evil spirits. It is a great testimony to the power of Christ when converted medicine men are used of God in the ministry of deliverance.

The high-profile deliverances at Navajo Mountain resulted in revival. Hundreds came to Christ out of the darkness of spirit worship. The miracle of exorcism performed in the name of Jesus Christ resulted in more than sensationalism—it demonstrated the victory of Christ in such a way that the Native people understood.

In those tribes where Christianity has made a significant impact there has been a victorious encounter with the powers of darkness by the Church. Some areas, both in North America and abroad, seem resistant to the gospel. The forces of Satan maintain their stranglehold through animism. New methods seem powerless to get through to the hearts of the people. The conclusion, I believe, is clear: The controlling demonic forces must be challenged before the harvest can be gathered in.

If missionaries and national Christians will intercede and claim the overcoming power of the Lord Jesus Christ, remarkable things can happen. I am convinced that in an atmosphere of animistic dominance, successful power encounters will precede the widespread ingathering of souls. Deliverance is sometimes a significant dimension of evangelism. One wonders if any soul can be rescued from the clutches of Satan without a power encounter at some level.

Ten Biblical Principles for Effective Deliverance Ministry

The Word of God provides an objective and factual view of the hosts of hell and affirms that all believers may experientially and victoriously confront these dark forces because of Christ's triumph over them. Christians do best in battle when they appropriate basic biblical principles and take their place beside the winner—Christ Jesus, the Lord.

THE CHRISTIAN BOOK market today is flooded with "how-to" books on exorcism and other aspects of demonology. However, at the time the events recorded here took place, we did not have those resources and had very little experience.

When it became evident that we were actually dealing with a case of demon possession, we were at a loss to know how to proceed. Though it may sound simplistic, the Bible became our guidebook. Passages that in the past had little meaning came to life, providing us with the basic principles needed to successfully participate in such a ministry. When nothing seemed to work, time was taken to search the Scriptures for light on the situation. When we confronted a blank wall, as we often did, the Holy Spirit always directed us to some word of truth that solved the problem. The New Testament, we believed, was the best textbook on the subject. I still believe that today.

The epistles lay the theological foundation for deliverance and relate it to the whole of biblical doctrine. Paul had a sound understanding of power encounters and instructed the Church in the importance of spiritual preparation for such encounters regardless of their severity.

The team also studied the numerous exorcistic details in the four Gospels, reading them again and again to receive insight and instruction. With the methods of Christ as our model, we were able to develop a deliverance methodology.

Those of us involved in the actual exorcism process found the manifestations of the spirits to be alarming. The violence, convulsions, frothing at the mouth and loud cries were disturbing. But after examining the manifestations in the Gospels, we discovered that what we were witnessing was similar to the New Testament accounts of demon possession.

For instance, in the most extreme biblical case, the demoniac of Gadara was so violent that at times all efforts to restrain him failed. He easily escaped by breaking the chains that had been placed on him (Mark 5:4).

Again, in Mark 9, the father of the possessed boy described there relates an account of the behavior induced by the mute demon. He said, " . . . whenever it seizes him, it throws him down; he foams at the mouth, gnashes his teeth, and becomes rigid" (9:18). The demons related to animism, we discovered, also tended to be violent.

Thankfully, the biblical records assured us that we were not hallucinating, but that what we were seeing was real. Observing Christ's manner of dealing with these manifestations helped us to get perspective. He was always calm in the presence of such behavior and used His divine authority to control the circumstances around Him. It was overwhelmingly evident that Christ did not fear the spirits. Rather, they feared Him and correctly protested the threatened loss of control over their victim.

The result of our study of the Scriptures during the heat of those battles was the discovery of ten basic biblical principles for effective deliverance ministry.

Principle One: Ask the Question

When a demon manifested itself during our first session with Lorna, the Lord drew our attention to First John 4:1-3:

> Beloved, do not believe every spirit,
> but test the spirits, whether they are of

God; because many false prophets have gone out into the world. By this you know the Spirit of God: every spirit that confesses that Jesus Christ has come in the flesh is of God, and every spirit that does not confess that Jesus Christ has come in the flesh is not of God. And this is the spirit of the Antichrist, which you have heard was coming, and is now already in the world.

Responding to this clear directive, we confronted the demon with the question, "Did Jesus Christ come in the flesh?" It responded with a clear "no." We discovered that when a spirit is tested and responds negatively according to the criteria, it is evidence that one is dealing with a true case of demon possession.

Sometimes symptoms and manifestations occur as a result of a mental or chemical condition in the body. Exorcism will not help relieve chemically induced symptoms nor will it cure mental illness. Of course, Christ can heal such conditions in answer to prayer and anointing with oil. But when an indwelling spirit denies that Christ is come in the flesh, the appropriate method is to cast it out in the name of the Lord Jesus Christ. (Some spirits may respond positively to the test question in an

effort to remain undetected. When a positive answer is given, one should simply continue to command the spirit until it answers truthfully.)

Some spirits, even after responding negatively to
the test, resisted leaving. This puzzled us until we
saw that Jesus in the incident of the demoniac of
Gadara required the demon to give its name *after* it
showed resistance. Mark's Gospel says, "For He
said to him, 'Come out of the man, unclean spirit!'
Then He asked him, 'What is your name?' And he
answered, saying, 'My name is Legion; for we are
many'" (Mark 5:8-9).

The Gospels do not record that Jesus always
asked the name of the demon, but in the event of
obvious multiple possession, Christ called for the
name. That became a key to our case. Once the
demon spoke his name, he was exposed and became more vulnerable, less resistant. This procedure proved helpful in facilitating the deliverance.

Principle Two:
Take Believer's Authority

From the first day of dealing with this case we
based our authority to do the work on Luke 9:1-2:
"Then He called His twelve disciples together and
gave them power and authority over all demons,
and to cure diseases. He sent them to preach the

kingdom of God and to heal the sick." Christ conferred both power and authority upon the twelve
founding apostles. The same was given to the seventy, indicating that the Church was empowered
for the ministry of deliverance.

That authority has never been revoked. It only
ceases in the face of unbelief. The history of revival
shows the association of a pure, Spirit-filled Church
and the credentials to deliver the bound in Christ's
name. When the Church is on fire with the flame
of the Spirit, the power of first-century Christianity
is once again freely exercised.

In another scenario, Jesus cast the evil spirit out
of a man in the synagogue in Capernaum. The demon cried out and Jesus commanded him to be
quiet. Jesus not only had authority to expel the demon—He had complete authority over its actions.
The Scriptures go on to say that the spirit convulsed him. There are four other incidents where
unclean spirits convulsed their victims when Jesus
commanded them to leave (Mark 1:26; 9:26; Luke
9:39; 9:42).

We found that the authority of the believer follows a similar pattern. When demons would become noisy, making it difficult to deal with the
person, it was possible to command them in
Christ's name to be quiet. The more we examined
the biblical accounts of Jesus casting out demons,

the more we realized the importance of placing our trust in the finished work of Christ and in the present demonstration of His power. Rather than being distracted by the manifestations of the demons, we persisted in using the authority vested in the Name above all names to control the situation.

This power and authority to cast out demons is not inherent in the Christian but is derived from Christ by faith. Jesus warned the early disciples not to rejoice in their authority over demons but to rejoice that their names were written in heaven (Luke 10:20). In order to maintain a proper perspective, contemporary disciples too must focus on Christ and our relationship to Him through biblical salvation. We are best equipped to take authority over demons when our hearts are overflowing with joy at the triumph of Christ crucified, risen and enthroned in glory. Christians do best in any battle when they stand alongside the winner, Christ Jesus the Lord.

The Power of Jesus' Name

No study of the biblical method of exorcism, including believers' authority, would be complete without a consideration of the power of Jesus' name. Jesus told His disciples they would cast out demons in His name. However, its use is theological, not methodological.

The name of Christ represents His character and

His power. It is glorious in the eyes of heaven, awesome in the eyes of saints, the most fearful thing in the universe in the eyes of the powers of darkness. His name is one of a kind, with no challenger among men or angels or demons. It is no small matter to invoke the name of Christ. But I repeat, the use of His name is theological, not methodological.

Satan also recognizes the power in that name and, with the wave of false teachings so pervasive today, it frequently happens that spirits will give their name as Jesus and/or Christ. Nonetheless, it is a false spirit speaking. Confronting the spirit with the name of the Lord Jesus Christ, Son of the Most High God will immediately expose the evil spirit for what it is.

The authority to exorcise evil spirits in the name of Christ is conferred upon believers for His glory. Such a supernatural act witnesses to the supreme power of the glorified Son of God. All of the combined intelligence of mankind could not produce such a cure for human bondage.

Although a human instrument is used, exorcism is a divine work. The Christian who engages in this ministry must do so with humility and total dependence on Christ. Using the name of Jesus Christ to cast out demons is a sacred trust.

Neither is the name of Christ to be used as a

magic formula. His name is given as the credential of heaven for the work of ministry to the bound. Let us not be mistaken: The demons know that name and they know its significance. It is also evident that they know when that name is being used by those not worthy of ministering for the Lord Jesus Christ. The itinerant Jewish exorcists in Ephesus attempted to invoke Jesus' name and were overcome by the demon-possessed person. They had no personal relationship to Jesus and therefore had no right to use His name (Acts 19:13-17).

There is something about ministering in the name of Christ that puts our Christian profession on the line. It is a great object lesson in spiritual integrity. If we undertake to walk on the borderland of the supernatural we must do so with a pure heart. The glory of Christ must be the end in view.

Philippians 2:5-11 was read aloud many times during those early deliverance sessions. A major emphasis in this explanation of Christ's incarnation is the prominence of His name. The Father has exalted Him above every name in heaven, on earth and in the realm of spirits. At His name all are to bow, be they human beings or angels or demons. Since the spirit world is aware of the power of His name, those who deal with that world should keep in mind the glorious power and influence of the name of the Lord Jesus Christ. His blessed name is a refuge for the saint in warfare and at the same time a mighty weapon in the battle.

Binding and Loosing

Another powerful weapon given to Christian believers is the authority to bind and loose. One who undertakes the ministry of deliverance should remember that though Satan is a defeated foe he *is* a "strong man." Jesus called the attention of His followers to this fact and instructed them in how to deal with it. "Or how can one enter a strong man's house and plunder his goods, unless he first binds the strong man? And then he will plunder his house" (Matthew 12:29). The idea of loosing is implied in this verse when the strong man is bound and his goods plundered. Plundering is the equivalent of loosing. It sets the goods free from his control. However, Jesus clearly states the principles of loosing in Matthew 18:18.

Loosing one who lives under the bondage of evil spirits requires the presence and power of the Stronger Man. In the name of the strongest, our Lord Jesus Christ, we have authority to bind the strong man and loose the victim. This is not an empty ritual, but the application of Christ's victory by faith to a given situation of spiritual bondage. The blood-bought and Spirit-born have through Christ the power to bind and loose.

While there are other usages of the idea of binding and loosing, in the context of Matthew 12 it refers to exorcism.

There have been many times when it was necessary to bind the spirit because it insisted on violent manifestations or other means to hinder the deliverance process. Others demons that came on the scene as reinforcements were also bound. But the worker must renounce any notion that he or she has the power to bind and loose. It is an authority exercised by faith in Christ's eternal triumph over all the powers of evil.

At the very beginning of the deliverance process it is helpful to pray for the binding of the strong man and the loosing of the victim. Christ is glorified by the dividing of the spoils of such a battle. Every true deliverance is a powerful witness to the reality of Christ's resurrection, ascension and enthronement in glory. The Spirit-filled Christian, by the authority of Christ, *can* strip the strong man and spoil his goods. What a great miracle takes place when a captive soul is thus set free!

The Power of the Holy Spirit

A third aspect of our authority as believers is the power of the Holy Spirit. Christ's opponents accused Him of casting out demons by the power of Beelzebub. He countered with the argument that Satan does not cast out Satan. If he did, his kingdom would collapse. He then asked by whom the Jews cast out demons and revealed that He cast out demons by the Holy Spirit (Matthew 12:28). Christ said that to cast out demons by the Holy Spirit indicated that the kingdom of God had come to them.

If the perfect, sinless, divine Son of God cast out demons by the Holy Spirit, then it must be assumed if His followers cast out demons they must also do so by the Holy Spirit. Without the power of the Spirit of God, the ministry of deliverance will fail. Those who engage in it must remember that they are only servants carrying out the Master's orders with the Master's credentials.

Principle Three:
Count on Divine Protection

While engaged in the work of deliverance, there is danger in giving into the suggestion of the enemy that there could be devastating consequences to this ministry. During the long days and nights of this particular case, there were times when the workers were ready to give up rather than face possible personal danger. Once again, it was the Word of God that quieted our hearts.

The most assuring passage was Luke 10:17-20. The seventy disciples sent out by Jesus to preach the gospel, heal the sick and cast out demons returned to report this experience.

> Then the seventy returned with joy, saying, "Lord, even the demons are subject to us in Your name." And He said to them, "I saw Satan fall like lightening from heaven. Behold, I give you the authority to trample on serpents and scorpions, and over all the power of the enemy, and nothing shall by any means hurt you. Nevertheless do not rejoice in this, that the spirits are subject to you, but rather rejoice because your names are written in heaven."

The danger is not in carrying out a ministry of deliverance, but in doing so with inadequate preparation and with a spirit of presumption. Christ provides for the protection of His people against the strategies of Satan and his forces. Christians need to remember the truth that greater is the One who is in them than the one (the devil) who is in the world (1 John 4:4). The apostle John in his first epistle said, "We know that whoever is born of God does not sin; but he who has been born of God keeps himself, and the wicked one does not touch him" (5:18).

The regenerate person, by faith and obedience, maintains a pure heart, giving no ground to the enemy. John Bengel says in his treatment of First John 5:18, "The regenerate is not ruined from without. The wicked one approaches as a fly does to a candle; but he does not injure him, he does not even touch him."[1] Christ is our shield and defense. In His loving care it is safe to minister deliverance in His exalted name.

It must, however, be remembered that to undertake this work with unconfessed sin and deliberate disobedience in one's life leaves one open to the enemy's attack. To engage the battle with curiosity about the demons and what they say or do is also dangerous. Equally foolhardy is attempting the ministry in one's own strength. Precautions are necessary because the powers of darkness are very powerful. A.W. Tozer warned that "Satan has been in the business of intimidating and silencing and oppressing the people of God for a long, long time."[2] But of one thing God's children can be sure: The Lord Jesus Christ is all-powerful and in Him is total victory.

Another dimension of the believer's protection against the attacks of the enemy is the armor of God. Many times when our bodies were numb from weariness, our minds dulled by hours of intense warfare, what comfort and uplift came from reading Ephesians 6:10-20! To claim by faith each piece of the armor changed the odds very quickly. This passage was a fresh reminder of the nature of the problem. We were not dealing with human flesh and blood, but with experienced, powerful, clever, subtle, persistent forces intent upon evil. It was good to know that the victory over them is based on truth, righteousness, gospel peace, salvation, the Word of God and faith. It is not some new insight that brings deliverance, but the consistent affirmation of the foundational truth of Christ's redemption.

There is a strange paradox in Paul's account of the armor for Christ's warriors. In Ephesians 6:15, Paul uses the phrase "and having shod your feet with the preparation of the gospel of peace." How did the word "peace" get into the discussion of a foot soldier's armor? The answer to that question teaches us what it means to be a good soldier of Jesus Christ. To put it simply—God's best soldier is a person of peace. He or she enjoys peace with God and the peace of God. The practical result of that spiritual relationship is perfect inner peace through Christ in the heat of the worst battle.

Principle Four: Pursue the Victory

We had to ask ourselves why this case was taking

so long. The biblical models of exorcism did not seem to indicate extended struggles. We eventually reached the conclusion that we must look to the doctrinal sections of the New Testament rather than the historical narrative to answer this question.

Paul's discussion of the armor of God indicates that when believers struggle with the powers of evil they must simply stand by faith. Such a stance eventually brings the victory. The reason for the struggle may be that larger issues are at stake. This particular event was tied to a major power encounter that would tear down a stronghold of demonic activity.

Paul's teaching in Ephesians 6 also shows the intensity of spiritual warfare, that perseverance is required in order to gain the victory. Victory is assured. Knowing that he or she will eventually win, the believer takes his or her stand on the sure Word of God which is a powerful weapon against the onslaughts of the enemy. Often in the heat of the battle we found it helpful to gird ourselves by reading the Word of God aloud and affirming its truth. While it fed the faith of the deliverance team and enabled them to persist in the battle, it also had a marked effect upon the demons.

The apostle John revealed the secret for overcoming Satan and his forces. In Revelation chapter 12, John describes a war in heaven in which Satan was cast to the earth. This scene is followed by a declaration that the kingdom of God and the power of His Christ have come. On the basis of the divine victory, the apostle says of the believers: "And they overcame him [Satan] by the blood of the Lamb and by the word of their testimony, and they did not love their lives to the death" (Revelation 12:11).

Victory in spiritual warfare rests first upon the blood atonement made by Jesus Christ at the cross. Christ is the Lamb of God and His blood is precious to all who understand redemption. At the cross Christ was successful in the total defeat of the powers of darkness. There the prophecy given by God the Father regarding the triumph of His Son over Satan was fulfilled: "And I will put enmity between you and the woman, and between your seed and her Seed; He shall bruise your head, and you shall bruise His heel" (Genesis 3:15).

When Jesus died and shed His blood, the devil was mortally wounded. There is no cure for his wound. With his power essentially gone, he now operates as a usurper. Paul confirms this in Colossians: "Having disarmed principalities and powers, He made a public spectacle of them, triumphing over them in it" (2:15). The powers of hell thought the cross to be their victory, but they were soon to learn that the suffering Savior had won the battle. What the demons intended to be the shame of Jesus turned out rather to be His glory and their shame.

All of us involved with this extended case of demon possession had a head knowledge of these biblical concepts, but they were only theological premises until our exposure to the reality of actual combat with the powers of darkness. Suddenly these Scripture texts were providing the strength and help we needed most, illuminating our minds with insight and instruction, enabling us to press on.

Principle Five: Discern Deception

Over the eight months that it took to gain complete deliverance for Lorna, all of us learned much about the skill of the evil spirits in the art of deception. Like their master Satan, they were proficient liars. They often attempted to engage the exorcists in conversation by offering all kinds of information. It very often proved to be false. (The evil spirits mentioned in Scripture told the truth when Christ questioned them. The problem we are addressing here is the initiation and control by demons of the subject matter.) On one occasion they pretended to leave and then laughed mockingly when we assumed a victory had been gained. At other times they pretended to be the Holy Spirit and told us that the young lady was delivered. Some workers became ensnared by this device. Obviously, discernment was needed.

As the weeks went by, a degree of discernment came from experience (Hebrews 5:14). This, of course, did not replace the need for supernatural discernment such as the gift of discerning of spirits included in Paul's list of spiritual gifts (1 Corinthians 12:10). There were times when the Holy Spirit gave this gift to some in our group, allowing them to immediately expose the deception of the manifesting demon. The practical effect was always a quick and easy expulsion of the demon.

At other times the person with the gift of discerning of spirits would detect the name of the evil spirit. This occurred when very stubborn spirits refused to give their names. Once the spirit's name was revealed, it would leave immediately. The gift of discerning of spirits seemed to be manifest only in times of great need and confusion.

Principle Six: Resist the Enemy

By searching the Scriptures we became convinced of the need to resist the devil and all his forces. This biblical principle is not only essential for the ministry of deliverance, but it is a frequent need in the daily walk of the Christian. The admonition of the apostle James is applicable: "Therefore submit to God. Resist the devil and he will flee from you. Draw near to God and He will draw near to you. Cleanse your hands, you sinners; and purify your hearts, you double-minded" (James 4:7-8).

There is no way to resist the devil in the flesh. One must first humbly submit to God and then draw near for cleansing and purification. Those who encounter the powers of darkness with triumph are those who forsake double-mindedness and fully yield to Christ. Cleansed and engulfed in the presence of God, the believer is empowered to resist the devil and his cohorts. Resisting is a conscious stand of faith against the thoughts, ways and workings of the evil spirits and their master the devil. It is a state of mind one must maintain in any encounter with the powers of darkness.

Peter discusses the subject of resisting the devil in chapter 5 of his first epistle. As did James, Peter urges the importance of a right relationship to Christ as the first prerequisite to successfully resisting Satan. Both James and Peter emphasize the need for a humble spirit in those who undertake such resistance.

Peter anticipated the tactics of the enemy when he said,

> Casting all your care upon Him, for He cares for you. Be sober, be vigilant; because your adversary the devil walks

> about like a roaring lion, seeking whom he may devour. Resist him, steadfast in the faith, knowing that the same sufferings are experienced by your brotherhood in the world. (1 Peter 5:7-9)

The enemy will attack the Christian with uncertainty, fear, weariness with the struggle and the insidious suggestion that God doesn't really care for His own. Peter was saying that when such negative and untrue thoughts begin, one cannot be passive. Action needs to be taken immediately. The believer must put up the shield of faith and resist steadfastly every clever attack of the devil.

Perhaps the most graphic description we have of resisting the devil comes from the writings of A.W. Tozer. His famous sermon *I Talk Back to the Devil* puts this concept into terms we understand:

> . . . God never meant for us to be kicked around like a football. He wants us to be humble and let Him do the chastening when necessary. But when the devil starts tampering with you, dare to resist him!
>
> I stand for believing in God and defying the devil—and our God loves that kind of courage among His people.[3]

We must take care that our "back talk" is on the sure ground of Christ's triumph over Satan. The devil flees when the godly talk back.

Principle Seven: Pray and Fast

A few demons encountered in Lorna were very strong and refused to leave when commanded. This puzzled the team. So we went to the Scriptures for light on the problem. Jesus' words to His disciples in Mark 9:29 enlightened us: "This kind can come out by nothing but prayer and fasting."[4] The disciples had been unable to cast out a spirit from a boy greatly tormented from early childhood. Jesus commanded the demon to leave, and even then it resisted to the end by throwing the child into a convulsion.

Our team on some occasions was criticized for its seeming inability to get instant deliverance. After reflection on Jesus' words to His disciples, we concluded that when we faced such strong demons we would resort to fasting and prayer. At times the battle continued for up to fifty-eight hours. But, in every instance, full deliverance came.

Those extended times of waiting on God brought untold blessing to all who participated. We were no longer alarmed at the idea that some spirits could put up such strong resistance. Christ *is* the victory; He has no need to *win* the victory over Satan and his forces. The temporary resistance of the demons, we learned, could be compared to the devil roaring like a lion—defeated, but hoping by his grandiose deception to hold his ground a bit longer.

Principle Eight: Sing and Praise

The singing of hymns with deep theological content was a daily routine. It became a part of the process just like prayer. The content of the hymns was important. Most focused on the blood of Christ or His resurrection from the dead. Each day we sang all the verses of "Oh, for a Thousand Tongues." Again and again we sang "There Is a Fountain Filled with Blood." It is of interest to note that these hymns provided great encouragement to the workers and at the same time produced great agitation in the evil spirits. Songs that exalted Christ or spoke of the blood and the resurrection were the most effective.

Even though these sessions were heavy experiences, there were times when the joy of the Lord would sweep over us and we would praise Him audibly. Psalm 149 became our favorite reading on these occasions. The psalmist says, "Let the saints be joyful in glory" (149:5). He also said, "Let the high praises of God be in their mouth" (149:6). The psalm goes on to describe the judgment of God on the enemies of righteousness and how the saints are a part of that process. He closes the psalm with the declaration, "This honor have all His saints" (149:9). (By "honor" is meant the privilege to be the instrument of Christ acting with the authority of Christ to overcome the power of the evil one.)

Singing and reading Psalms interspersed with shouts of joy dealt staggering blows to the forces of evil. Joy seemed foreign to them. The praise of God filled them with fear. What an insight into the misery that characterizes the domain of darkness! The pure, heartfelt praise of the Lord Jesus Christ, we found, reverberates to the very center of Satan's kingdom. We can shout with Paul, "But thanks be to God, who gives us the victory through our Lord Jesus Christ" (1 Corinthians 15:57).

Principle Nine: Cast out the Demon

After counseling, instruction, prayer, fasting, singing, praising and testing the spirits, the task of exorcism is yet to come. The goal of the deliverance process is to free the victim completely of the demons' presence and power. Jesus called this aspect of the ministry "casting out demons." The concept can be best understood by examining the Greek verb *ekballo*. The lexicon gives as the first meaning of this word—"to drive out, expel, throw out more or less forcibly."

Since the demon has strongholds in the personality, it will not yield that place unless forced to do so by a superior power. To make the demon relinquish its hold and leave requires both power and authority. Christ conferred on those He delegated to cast out demons the authority *and* the power to do so. Christians who undertake this work must be clothed with power from on high. They must also by faith see themselves seated in heavenly places in Christ Jesus. The Holy Spirit is the source of power and the enthroned Christ is the place of authority.

To be precise, Jesus cast out demons by commanding them to leave the possessed person. That act implied that the demon was to give up all control of the individual and leave. Casting out the demon is the high point in the whole process of deliverance. The conflict is brought to completion by expelling the evil spirit and consequently freeing the victim.

The phenomena of how demons leave is a study in itself. The New Testament records show that convulsions, frothing at the mouth and loud cries occurred in some cases when the demons left.

These actions seem to be one last but minor act of rebellion even though the demons know full well they have been defeated. Such manifestations do not always take place. Some demons leave quietly, witnessed only by an evident sense of release of the possessed person.

Principle Ten: Discern between Healing and Exorcism

As Lorna's deliverance progressed, physical and psychological symptoms were observed that gave the team concern. It was the writings of Luke in his Gospel and the Acts that gave insight into this need. In Luke chapter 6, the evangelist records the story of a large gathering of people from Jerusalem, Judea and the coastal cities of Tyre and Sidon. Many sick and possessed people were present. The Scriptures say that Jesus healed all the sick and then state that He healed all those tormented with unclean spirits. There were no doubt persons suffering various levels of demonic activity, but most certainly there were those who were actually possessed. Luke, in this passage, makes deliverance a healing ministry.

The Lord Jesus knew the difference between demon possession and mental illness. He healed the mentally ill and drove the demons out of the possessed. That distinction is important in our time as well. Care must be taken to determine the real cause of the manifesting symptoms. Some symptoms of possession are similar to symptoms of mental illness or chemical imbalances. If care is not taken to make a proper diagnosis, the person could be traumatized by the process of misapplied exorcism.

It is sometimes advisable to learn the medical history of the individual or it may be wise to ask if the person has had a psychiatric evaluation. If the symptoms have no physical or psychiatric basis, there is a strong likelihood that the problem is of demonic origin. Since we do not have perfect knowledge like the Lord Jesus, we should learn all we can about the activities of the individual and determine if there is any ground for demonic invasion in his or her experience. Some teachers on this subject seem to imply that demons have ready access to human beings and one can therefore be easily possessed. That position presents the frightening possibility that one could be possessed accidently. Neither the Scriptures nor the experiences of over fifty years in dealing with possession brings me to that conclusion.

The demon-possessed person not only needs the exorcism of the evil spirit, but healing from the devastating effects of possession. Physical ailments of all kinds show up in possessed persons. Sometimes these symptoms disappear when the spirit(s) is (are) cast out. In other cases, the physical condition may linger. Prayer for healing—not exorcism—should be offered in such cases.

Luke makes another reference to healing in the context of the demonic in Acts 10:38. He reports that Jesus healed all who were oppressed of the devil. The psychological effects of possession also need healing. Victims may find themselves depressed and feeling mentally unstable. The ability to think clearly may be impaired. Thank God, the healing touch of Christ can bring restoration.

After learning these concepts, special prayer for healing of mind and body was offered during Lorna's deliverance. The results were remarkable. She seemed like a new person. Her emotions were stable. Her mind became alert. She memorized Scripture passages and displayed above-average intellect. Her prayers were powerful. It seemed that her true personality was being discovered for the first time. She began reading large portions of the Bible each day and showed a clear understanding of what she read.

Conclusion

• **The revealed Scriptures are wholly true and give an objective, factual view of the powers of darkness.** Here we learn the nature of Satan and demons. Their history is recorded so one can understand their fall and their subsequent rebellion against God and God's people. The Bible also shows the divine limitations on the activity of the evil powers. They are given realms of authority. Satan is the god of this world. The whole world order including government, culture and lifestyle is energized by these evil personalities. The system is the product of an intelligent but morally twisted mind.

• **Spiritual warfare is much more than dealing with exorcism.** The Christian lives in this alien system and must confront its evil influence daily. The spiritual resources available to the exorcist are needed by all Christians. One great benefit of dealing with demon possession is the experiential realization that Jesus Christ has triumphed over the hosts of hell and that victory is applied today whenever God's people appropriate it by faith.

•

• **The Word of God is a reliable guide for the ministry of deliverance.** The methods of Christ set forth in the Gospels and the same methods used by the first-century Christians are equally effective today. Deliverance from demon possession is redemptive. It was an integral part of the overall ministry of Christ. He delegated the work to His

Church. Wherever the gospel message of redemption is fully preached in the world, deliverance from demonic bondage will take place.

• **The ministry of deliverance demonstrates who the winner is in this conflict.** There is a sense in which the phenomenon of demon possession is a graphic and public display of the larger but sometimes hidden conflict with evil and the intelligence behind it. Demon possession displays the violent, insane, hideous side of evil, but the ministry of deliverance provides convincing proof that Jesus Christ is the King of kings and Lord of lords who now reigns and shall reign forever and ever.

Thank God there is in the gospel of Christ release for the possessed. It is still possible for even the most demented to be made whole and sit clothed and in their right minds.

Endnotes

[1] John A. Bengel, *Gnomon of the New Testament*, Vol. 1 (Edinburgh: T. & T. Clarke, 1843), p. 153.

[2] A.W. Tozer, *I Talk Back to the Devil* (Camp Hill, PA: Christian Publications, 1990), p. 4.

[3] Ibid., pp. 15-16.

[4] ". . . and fasting" is not in all manuscripts.

CHAPTER SEVEN

Preparation for the Battle

The resurgence of animism in this century in so-called Christian countries of the world is a clear call to the Church to offer deliverance to the captives in Christ's name. Only a pure, Spirit-empowered Church can triumphantly confront the domain of deception, darkness, demons, death and damnation.

ALTHOUGH THE MINISTRY of deliverance has never completely disappeared through the centuries of Church history, it has been renewed most often when the Church is in a state of revival. At the cutting edge of world evangelism people are being delivered from demons at the end of the twentieth century just as they were in the first century. The resurgence of animism in the so-called Christian countries of the world is a clear call to the Church to offer, in Christ's name, deliverance to the captives. This is not a fad or a new trend. The ministry of deliverance is a mighty work of Christ which He is carrying out through His people to set free the many in our modern world who live in bondage to evil spirits.

But this ongoing battle requires vigilance. Paul warned the Christians of his day not to be ignorant of Satan's devices (2 Corinthians 2:11). Today, as then, believers need teaching and preparation for entering into the ministry of deliverance.

Preparation Based on Sound Doctrine

Knowledge of the truth is the best antidote to the strategies of the demonic forces. The foundation for the whole process of spiritual preparation is sound doctrine. The believer must know the truth that sets people free. His or her theology must be straight regarding Jesus Christ, the Bible, the blood of Christ, divine authority, the personalities behind evil and their ultimate doom, the person and work of the Holy Spirit and the triumph of Christ through His death, resurrection, ascension, enthronement and coming kingdom.

For a Christian to become subjective with regard to spiritual warfare is disastrous. What will hold up in the hour of battle is the objective truth revealed in God's Word. The secret of standing in the heat of the fight is the girdle of truth. The entire satanic system is built on lies and deception. It cannot stand against the truth. The neglect of teaching sound doctrine over the past two or three decades has left God's people vulnerable. Those who serve in this ministry must have an intelligent grasp of basic doctrine. The uncertain feelings of existential experience will not cut it in this war.

John Bunyan offers a reminder of the Christian's

weakness when he or she confronts the evil powers in his or her own strength. Bunyan's *Pilgrim's Progress* recounts the painful failures of those who neglected the truth and became victims of the enemy rather than victors over him. In every instance they ignored or strayed from the truth.[1] Because of the nature of spiritual warfare, those in the ministry of deliverance need solid teaching which establishes them in the Word.

The Eschatalogical Dimension to Spiritual Warfare

There is also an eschatalogical dimension to spiritual warfare. The New Testament epistles warn believers that the spirit of Antichrist is already at work in the world. A part of the apostle Paul's rationale for the pursuit of holiness is based on the stepped-up demonic activity as the time for Christ's return draws near.

In the second chapter of Thessalonians, Paul shows the intensity of the mystery of lawlessness in the last days. He describes the saints as those who receive the love of the truth and the lost as those who do not receive the love of the truth. It is the Christian's love for the unchanging truth that keeps him or her surefooted in the battle.

In Second Thessalonians chapter 3, Paul urges his friends to pray that the word of the Lord may

have free course and that both he and his brethren
be delivered from unreasonable and wicked persons who are under satanic delusion. The apostle
follows this discussion with a summary statement
on God's provision for His soldiers engaged in battle: "But the Lord is faithful, who will establish
you and guard you from the evil one" (2 Thessalonians 3:3). The soldiers of the cross are made ready
for war by the deeper work of God's grace which
establishes them. They have settled their allegiance
to Christ, consecrated their whole being to Him,
and they are clothed with power by the Holy
Spirit. This verse essentially says that God in His
faithfulness establishes us.

It goes without saying that pastors, teachers and
fellow Christians are also a part of the process, but
it is God who matures and settles us in Christ. It is
God who guards believers from all the onslaughts
of the evil one. The powers of darkness will do
anything they can to keep believers from the ministry of deliverance. They will especially attempt to
intimidate Christians with fear. The victory over
fear is the settled assurance that Christ has defeated Satan and all his forces. The Scriptures state
that God will protect us. An essential step in the
preparation for this work is absolute trust in the
promises of God and in Christ's commission to cast
out demons in His name.

As surely as Christ sent His Church into the world to preach the gospel, He provided the power and authority to do the job. The whole of the Christian life and ministry requires the power of God. Christ's answer to this need is the coming of the Holy Spirit, not just to the corporate body of the Church but to each individual person in the body of Christ. When Jesus commissioned the Church He reminded her that the promise of the Father was about to come upon them. He said, "You shall be baptized with the Holy Spirit not many days from now" (Acts 1:5). Ten days later the Spirit came upon the waiting 120 disciples. The record is clear—those weak, trembling Christians became dynamos of spiritual power. No longer afraid, they stood for Christ against incredible odds. The same miracles that attended the ministry of Christ attended their ministry and the witness of this Spirit-filled Church shook the Roman Empire to its foundations.

By all the laws of group dynamics they should have been wiped out in a matter of weeks. But the Church not only survived—she triumphed over every foe arrayed against her through the power of the risen Christ. The modern Church with all her methods, money, technology and education must learn that all of these "benefits" are helpless against the onslaught of the powers of hell. At this point the Church must fall on her knees and cry to God for the outpouring of the Holy Spirit to equip her members with power from on high. As it was in the beginning, only the Spirit-filled person can do the work of delivering the bound in Jesus' name.

Pure Hearts a Necessity

All of Christ's servants need pure hearts, but particularly those who are engaged in deliverance ministry. Sin is the tap root of all spiritual problems, including demonic bondage. Those who confront the enemy must be clean, with everything under the blood.

An important aspect of this level of spirituality is death to the self-life. Nothing in the human heart is more like the devil than an uncrucified ego. We must cling to the cross until the last vestige of unsanctified self is dead. Christ can then indwell our lives and take up His throne there. A Christian who walks in the shared holiness of Christ assumes every ministry with confidence. Whatever is accomplished, he or she will say, "It is Christ in me."

The biblical preparation for deliverance ministry should include all these basics of true spirituality. But in addition to these broad steps of preparation are the immediate steps with each incident that arises: (1) Do not hurry into a deliverance situation; (2) take time for extended prayer and heart searching; (3) fast if possible; (4) engage in Spirit-empowered intercession; (5) particularly in animistic cases, seek God for discernment as to possible larger implications of the battle. The deliverance of the single victim of possession may well be the key to a family or a clan or a whole geographic area for the gospel.

The Church too often thinks of the ministry of deliverance as a compassionate act of mercy toward those who suffer at the hands of demons. It certainly is that, but it is much more. Jesus taught that deliverance is a confirmation of the truth and integrity of the gospel to those who reside in the darkness of spirit worship.

Supervision by Pastors and/or Elders

In some instances, the ministry of deliverance reaches a level of normalcy in the work of the Church. And so it ought to be. But after a few years it sometimes slips back into obscurity again because of excesses and a lack of balance. Deliverance is not a work for amateurs. Nor is it a mission for the curious. Such an undertaking should be supervised by the elders and pastoral leadership of a church. There is a tendency to make deliverance a counseling ministry apart from the church. That practice has its flaws.

The ideal way to carry out this responsibility is to have in the congregation a well-trained and godly ministry team under the direction of and amenable to the pastor(s) and elders. The combined discernment, experience, maturity and spiritual insight of the team helps to maintain balance in the execution of this work. The team will be a special target of the enemy and they should be surrounded with prayer. Through intercessory prayer, the whole church makes a contribution to their ministry.

Present the Gospel

It is advisable to present the gospel of Christ to those coming from spirit worship. In some cases the demons may manifest themselves to a point that one is immediately launched into the process of exorcism. But in most cases the victim is rational and the claims of Christ should be presented first. If the person renounces the spirits and confesses Christ, the exorcism will move more rapidly. Even in worst-case scenarios, it is usually possible after casting out one or two demons to deal with the individual about turning to Christ.

It is important that the presentation of the gospel to an animist be done with sensitivity to his or her culture and religious background. A cut-and-dried Western approach to evangelism may not work. If no one on the team has knowledge of the form of animism from which the victim comes, contact someone who has or is now working with that group. There is a place for common sense in the work of freeing the bound.

Read Books with a Sound Biblical Approach

The preparation for deliverance should include some solid reading. The market is flooded with books on demonology, but not all of them reflect a sound biblical approach. The bibliography at the end of this book provides a list of helpful books on both the theology and practice of deliverance. My book *Divine Healing, The Children's Bread* has a chapter on exorcistic procedures that may be helpful in training a ministry team. Another book of great value in teaching on this subject is J.A. MacMillan's *The Authority of the Believer.* For those dealing with animists, the work of John Nevius, renowned Presbyterian missionary to China and Mongolia, provides significant insights from his extended experience with several animistic cultures. This classic has been unequaled in its field for more than 100 years.

Implement Appropriate Follow-up

Many today, like the Thessalonians, are turning

from idols to serve the living God (1 Thessalonians 1:9-10) and coming to the Church for deliverance. For Westerners, the implications of such a radical change may not be immediately evident. The proper follow-up is critical. The ministry team will profit from training in discipleship designed for converted animists.

Another important aspect of follow-up relates to post-deliverance care. The victims of possession need special help in the first weeks after deliverance. They will find themselves harassed by the enemy and will need teaching on how to deal with his onslaughts. Instruction in consistent renouncing of the powers of darkness and all their works and ways will help the newly delivered to maintain victory.

Recently saved and delivered persons will also benefit from fellowship within a local church. Everything possible must be done to nurture these liberated souls. Time and effort will be needed to teach them how to have a daily devotional life and participate in the life of a church. The pastor may find it helpful to instruct the whole congregation as to how to relate to those who are attempting to enter the church family. Remember, the first person to see Jesus after the resurrection was Mary Magdalene out of whom He had previously cast seven demons. He did not see her as an oddity, but as a normal Christian. She had a place of respect among the first believers. In the same way, the Church today has an opportunity in the ministry of exorcism to exalt and praise the Lord Jesus Christ by opening its ranks to the newly delivered.

Learn How to Discern the Levels of Demonic Approach

The preparation of those who minister in this field of service should include a study of discernment. Because the demonization of human personalities is so complex one must be able to discern the various levels of demon approach. The examples in this book deal with actual possession, but the ministry team will likely encounter people suffering from various attacks of the enemy. In my opinion, exorcism is the process only for demon possession.

The plan of attack should await some discernment of the problem. If the victim is not troubled with loss of consciousness or physical manifestations or uncontrollable behavior, he or she is probably not possessed. If the person is extremely depressed and there is no established physical or psychological reason for the depression, it is likely the person is being oppressed by the powers of darkness. The possibility of mental illness should not be overlooked. If mental illness is suspected, advise the person to get a psychiatric evaluation. This will also explore any chemical problem that might be causing the symptoms.

Once it has been established that the problem is not psychological or medical, the person should receive biblical counseling, preferably by someone on the ministry team properly prepared for such a ministry. Intense prayer should accompany the counseling.

Maintain Unity within the Team

A successful deliverance team works in unity. By praying together and training together the team members come to a common ground on the theology and methodology of this kind of ministry.

One issue that often causes conflict is whether or not a Christian can be demon possessed. Many evangelical Christians categorically deny that possibility. But a growing number of evangelicals now believe that it can happen. From the days of the early Church it was a practice to test new converts preparing for baptism for the possibility of evil spirits lingering from their old life.[2] This was especially needful in light of their animistic background.

Most all the converts in the earliest stage of the Church were from animistic religions, with the exception of those from Judaism. When the Roman world became nominally Christian the work of the exorcist became less frequent. It should be noted that the office of exorcist is still maintained in the Catholic Church and to some extent in the Anglican Church.

The fact that the late first-century Church employed an exorcist in the catechetical team to prepare converts for baptism is significant. It implies that they believed it possible that these new converts from paganism could still be possessed and, if so, that it should be cared for before baptism. This confirms our experience among converted Native American animists: The church leadership often failed to explore the possibility of latent demonic problems. When these new believers came into an intense spiritual atmosphere the spirits became restless and soon exposed their presence. In Western culture the problem has a different cause. The proliferation of false cults has drawn many into the snare of a pseudo-religious experience.

Two passages in Paul's letters seem to imply the possibility of a Christian becoming demon possessed by giving ground to the enemy. In Second Corinthians 11:1-4 the apostle shares his concern that the believers in Corinth not lose their simplicity in Christ. He implies that spiritual adultery, the same analogy the prophets used in the Old Testament, would corrupt the believers who were espoused to Christ alone. He continues his argument by talking about his fear of Satan's subtle methods of spiritual corruption. He specifically mentions receiving "another Jesus" or "another spirit" or "another gospel" as the high points of danger. How could such things threaten the Christians' well-being if demon possession were not possible?

I have encountered numerous cases of possession that reflect the exact situation Paul describes—believers deceived by Satan so as to open their lives to demon control. It is not an accident. It happens because an informed person gives in to the devil's lie. Sin is *always* the ground of demon possession.

I have found that those who claim to be confessing Christians are possessed for one of three reasons: (1) They were possessed at the time of conversion and the problem through ignorance was not dealt with; (2) they slipped into sin after conversion, covering it up for an extended period of time instead of confessing it; and (3) they gave themselves over to false religious experiences.

Ministry teams will have to grapple with this issue. Those who reject the possibility usually do so on the basis of their allegiance to a closed system of theology. But like it or not—believe it or not—the people who seek your help often will profess to be saved. The problem then is no longer academic.

How we view the issue of the possibility of a believer being possessed will affect how we deal with the case. If you view the person as unsaved, you will seek their conversion in the deliverance process. If you see the person as a Christian, you will deal with their spiritual flaws and level of consecration as part of the deliverance. Those whose responsibility it is to train workers for this ministry will do well to discuss this issue carefully and prepare the team for encountering people who profess salvation yet show every evidence of demon possession.

Demon possession is a subject most people avoid. We would all agree that it can be a very disturbing experience to witness or to be involved in ministering to those who suffer this diabolical condition. But it has its positive sides. Demon possession confirms the accuracy of the Scriptures. Once you observe it, you discover that the biblical accounts do not differ from the phenomenon as it is today. You also see how the spirit world fears Christ and yields to His mighty power. Demon possession is a human affliction that can only be cured by the power and authority of Christ. Every true deliverance is a miracle.

In A.B. Simpson's study of Mark chapter 5, he makes a statement about demon possession that should be pondered by those who undertake a

ministry of deliverance. Simpson, commenting on
the violence and tendencies to self-destruction evi-
denced in the demoniac of Gadara, says, "This was
a little section of hell let loose on earth to give us a
glimpse of the world of darkness and despair."[3]
What a graphic description of demon possession!
It is a warning of the awful reality of the wicked
one and his dreadful domain of deception, darkness, demons, death and damnation.

Hell was made for the devil and his angels. People go there because they reject Christ and choose
Satan and his ways. In one sense, demon possession
is an object lesson of the anguish in hell. It is good
for Christians to witness this lesson because it can
move believers to win the lost and stir their hearts
to an uncompromising walk with Christ.

The massive resurgence of spirit worship means
that, for the Church, spiritual warfare has a whole
new battlefront. It also means that outreach for the
Church in this country will be, even more than in
the past, directed to animistic people. Spiritual
warfare must of necessity be a major concern in
evangelism and discipleship. A part of the gospel
proclamation is the release of the captive. Jesus
breaks every fetter and He sets men and women
free by His almighty power. He is the hope of
those who lie languishing in the bondage of demon
possession. The Church dare not be silent about

this aspect of Christ's victory nor should it be passive about the ministry of deliverance through Jesus Christ our Lord.

In this book there is no effort to introduce new methodology in the field of deliverance ministry. It is rather a clear call to spiritual awakening. The encounter with the powers of darkness faced by the modern Church is so overwhelming that only a pure and Spirit-empowered Church can meet it with triumph.

Let us, with deep humility and repentance, seek God for cleansing, the outpouring of the Holy Spirit and the equipping of the Church to fight a good fight until the moment we meet Christ in the air.

Endnotes

[1] John Bunyan, *Pilgrim's Progress* (Westwood, NJ: Barbour and Company, n.d.), pp. 58-71.

[2] Alexander Roberts and James Donaldson, "Constitution of the Apostles XXXIII," *The Ante-Nicene Fathers*, Vol. 7 (Grand Rapids, MI: Eerdmans, 1989), pp. 494-95.

[3] A.B. Simpson, *The Christ in the Bible Commentary*, Vol. 4 (Camp Hill, PA: Christian Publications, 1993), p. 220.

Sorting It Out, Keeping on Track

Fundamental to a sound ministry of deliverance is a sound theology of deliverance. It is time to sort out the various theories, methodologies and secular intrusions into detecting and overcoming demonic activity, and to reaffirm the theological and biblical basis of the deliverance ministry. Such a stance will keep us from drifting toward the fanatical fringe in matters of spiritual warfare.

THE RENEWED INTEREST in demonology and spiritual warfare has spawned many books dealing with these subjects. Not all of them are of equal value. Some are unsound theologically, while others have been overly innovative in their methodology. It is urgent that Church leaders develop a criteria for judging written works on demonology and deliverance ministry.

Since the books on this subject seem to ebb and flow with the interest level of the Christian community, there have been long periods when no useful books were written and the classics went out of print. Forty years ago, many spent considerable time and effort to acquire copies of the classic works on these doctrines. It is encouraging that a viable body of literature is now available.

Beginning in the 1960s, the evangelical Church took a fresh interest in the concept of the

Christian's encounter with the powers of darkness. What was happening in the culture no doubt prompted this new interest. The debut of rock music, Woodstock, youth rebellion and the use of drugs seemed to occur simultaneously with widespread demonic manifestations. Christians soon began to see the seriousness of this new and rather overwhelming display of demonic activity.

As a plethora of books came off the presses, "experts" offered to teach seminars in spiritual warfare. Believers in general were weak in their understanding of Satan and the demons and how they worked. They were equally uninformed as to the gospel's provisions for victory over the enemy through Christ. More works produced over the following decade dealt with the biblical teaching on demonology. And, in time, theologians began to compare notes with psychologists and psychiatrists.

Thousands of case studies eventually developed. It has been the study of case histories that has introduced a whole new dimension into the teaching of power encounter and how to deal with it. Case studies along with referrals to secular disciplines have tended to bring extensive extrabiblical input into the evangelical approach to demonology and deliverance ministry. There is a growing need for theologians to study this doctrine from a biblical perspective in order to maintain a balance in the complex area. Missiologists also have a role in keeping this teaching on track.

The most controversial theories have come out of the actual deliverance phenomena. Experience has sometimes been placed above Scripture, resulting in non-biblical methods. Among those new theories creating concern are the concepts of territorial spirits and the genealogical transmission of spirits (see Appendices B and C). A third questionable theory is the involuntary invasion of humans by demons. These ideas are gaining ground rather rapidly. In the light of trends, the time has come to reaffirm the biblical and theological basis of the deliverance ministry.

The waters have been further muddied by the renewed "signs and wonders" movement. This movement, though associated with a number of top-flight academically qualified people, is nevertheless flawed. The Third Wave Neo-Charismatics, while holding to classical Pentecostal views of demonology, have also been leaders in the non-biblical innovations in this field, such as the redefining of demon possession and surrounding it with an ambiguity that often leads to confusion. Trauma and other repercussions have resulted from the failure to detect the nature of demonic activity and to deal with it accordingly. To use the approach of exorcism with people who are not possessed can trigger both psychological and spiritual damage of serious proportions.

Before examining in more detail some of the tensions in the deliverance movement, it is essential to point out one more problem——-the interaction with psychologists and psychiatrists in deliverance. Some Christians have gone so far as to ask secular scientists to sit in on deliverance sessions. Such a practice indicates faulty assumptions as to the nature of exorcism. Exorcism is not now nor shall it ever be a medical matter. That is not to say that those who engage in this ministry have no concern with medical issues. If one suspects the victim has medical or psychological problems that may account for his or her behavior, then a Christian psychologist or psychiatrist should examine the person to determine if such conditions or imbalances exist. If the condition is medical, then exorcism would be harmful.

On the other hand, if the person has no medical cause for the condition and possession is actually established, then exorcism is the only relief for the condition. Demon possession yields only to the authority and power of Christ. The casting out of evil spirits is a supernatural work of God. There are Christian doctors, psychiatrists and psychologists involved in the ministry of deliverance who are fully committed to the biblical stance on deliverance.

The Practice of Interviewing Demons

Among the innovations in the methodology of deliverance is the practice of interviewing demons. Some of the concepts mentioned above result from this procedure. It is true that Jesus and the apostles did speak to demons, but there is no scriptural evidence they interviewed them for information about the victim's condition nor its causes. It is hardly debatable that demons do speak from possessed individuals. It was true in biblical times and it is true today. The question is: What kind of information do demons have and is it always reliable?

Demons like to talk and often use conversation as a ploy to divert the attention of the deliverance team from real issues at hand. Evil spirits will lie if it suits their agenda. They serve and are subject to the father of lies who is Satan. It should therefore not be surprising that demons use lying as a tactic in their effort to maintain mastery of the possessed person.

The person under the control of the demon—not the demon or demons—holds the key to the causes and ground of the possession. If the deliverance process is not moving well it is often because the victim is holding back something in his or her life that needs to be renounced. Rather than go to the demons for this information, go to the possessed person. Stop the exorcism and counsel with the individual as to possible unsurrendered areas.

It is not uncommon for persons in this condition to hold back information that has a bearing on the case. Encourage confession, repentance and renunciation of the sins or practices that gave the enemy a foothold. Have prayer with the person before resuming the exorcism. Should the person not want to cooperate with this procedure, end the session and suggest they think about the possibility of further need of confession. Urge them to contact the deliverance team as soon as they feel ready to resume the process. Persistent, intercessory prayer on the part of others can soon break such a stalemate. The possessed person must take responsibility for his or her sins.

Talking to the demons to learn the background and causes of possession has no biblical precedent. Nothing the demons might say is verifiable and they will lie in order to derail the deliverance team onto secondary issues if they can. In one instance that I can cite, a deliverance team was rather new at the task and engaged the spirits in conversation. Suddenly a spirit spoke saying that he was the Holy Spirit and that upon his coming all the evil spirits left.

The team was suspicious and asked if Christ had come in the flesh. The spirit responded in the positive and then began to quote Scripture at great length. He followed that demonstration with a rather striking sermonette on the ministry and work of the Holy Spirit. The deliverance team became convinced that this was the Holy Spirit and one of its members came to tell me of what he perceived to be a remarkable deliverance.

On entering the room, I disturbed the team by rebuking the spirit and commanding that it identify itself with its true name. The demon began to laugh and to blaspheme the name of the Lord. The members of the team were astounded. Some never fully recovered from that incident. Demons are not reliable sources of information. To engage them in that manner borders on the occult.

The Bible records only minimal accounts of demons speaking. The demons in biblical times were terrorized by the presence and the words of the Lord Jesus Christ. Their response was the same toward those who ministered in Christ's name. This has not changed. The incident of the Jewish exorcist that attempted to cast out demons in Christ's name makes clear the knowledge the demons have of Christ's triumph over them and the authority Christ gives His followers over them. When the Jewish exorcist attempted deliverance the evil spirit said, "Jesus I know, and Paul I know; but who are you?" (Acts 19:15).

The biblical doctrine of deliverance allows for no experimentation on the part of believers who engage in exorcism. It is always a battle between darkness and light. There is no light in the secular world nor in the world of evil spirits. Christ is exclusively the light that scatters the darkness. This truth is basic to any valid ministry of deliverance. The work of deliverance is to apply the victory of Calvary to the demonic manifestation and to do so in Christ's name and authority. The work of the victim is to be honest and open about the sin or sins responsible for the condition of bondage. Theologically, the ministry of deliverance is much more than the casting out of demons. Deliverance is more than an act of power—it is the spiritual transformation of the bound.

We are given in the Scriptures all we really need to know about the powers of darkness. The Scriptures provide ample light to detect demonic activity and to deal with it. The practice of interviewing demons is non-biblical and has the latent danger of deceiving those who engage in it.

The Transmission of Demons

Another new idea in deliverance work is the concept of the genealogical transmission of evil spirits. This teaching claims that demons are some-times transmitted from generation to generation in a given family. In many instances it is based on in-formation secured from interviews with demons. I find no biblical support for this idea. Certainly par-ents who engage in demonic worship expose their children and other family members to spirit influ-ence which could eventually lead to possession. But that cannot be described as "inheriting de-mons" which suggests the victim has no responsi-bility in their condition of possession (see Appendix C).

Some teach that demons can enter humans when and as they please. One teacher in this field speaks of what he calls the "involuntary entrance" of demons. He suggests that while one is sedated or unconscious demons could enter. These are as-sumptions with no basis in revealed Scripture.

How demons possess human beings is a critical issue. In Scripture the condition of possession re-lates to human action that opens the personality to demonic invasion. It is generally the victim's love of sin and his or her uncontrolled indulgence in it that allows the invasion of unclean spirits.

Demon possession is not just an unfortunate ac-cident. The demon possessed have given areas of their lives over to Satan. Sometimes the victim has made a deal with the spirits to receive power for his or her own purposes. He or she may want magical powers over other people or help in the gratification of their sins. The most glaring sin is breaking the first commandment: "You shall have no other gods before Me" (Exodus 20:3). Even though all animists are guilty of this sin, not everyone who worships a false god (or demon) is possessed. Only those who press on to know and communicate with the spirits are likely to be possessed. The giving of more and more ground to the enemy becomes the primary cause of their possession. Human sin is the ground of this diabolical condition.

During the spiritual awakening in Ephesus that gave birth to the Ephesian church, many animists were converted to Christ. The Scripture states that those who had engaged in magic and other forms of demon activity brought their occult books together and burned them (Acts 19:19). By this act they repented and renounced those wicked practices. The confrontation of the powers of hell by the gospel of Jesus Christ was evident. There were many delivered from possession during those days (19:12). It was evidently such a pervasive need that it required special miracles on the part of the apostle Paul. Christian exorcism was shown to be distinct from the so-called exorcisms of the sorcerers of Ephesus. Christian exorcism is unique in that it exalts Christ, is redemptive in nature and forthrightly deals with sin.

The Ground of Possession

Jesus in John 14:30 introduced the possibility of humans yielding ground to the enemy. Jesus said, "I will no longer talk much with you, for the ruler of this world is coming, and he has nothing in Me." Christ was without sin and Satan had no access to Him. Since mankind is sinful, the evil one takes advantage of our humanity. He cleverly seeks to deepen the ground given to him by human sin.

The intense desires of the carnal heart can lead to dangerous levels of yielding to Satan. Several examples come to mind. The desire to talk to dead loved ones has often eventuated in possession. The indulgence of gross immorality has been the path of demonic bondage for many a soul. Uncontrolled anger, like a moral cancer, can be the basis for the agonizing misery of control by evil spirits. Lying is a frequent ground of demon possession. False religious experience is another possible ground. I repeat: The ground of possession is the willful indulgence in sin. Because that is true, deliverance requires the victim to confess and forsake the ground of their possession.

Another New Testament passage that speaks to this subject is found in Ephesians 4:26-27: " 'Be

angry, and do not sin': do not let the sun go down
on your wrath, nor give place to the devil." Paul
warns the Ephesians of a real danger, that of giving
place to the devil. The New Testament teaches
that by one's own will and actions ground can be
surrendered. Satan is quick to take up that ground
and seek to strengthen his claim upon it. Christians need to take seriously this teaching, but so do
the unregenerate who, without such light, open
themselves to the enemy, sometimes to the extent
that the powers of darkness have easy ground for
possession.

The New Testament records two remarkable incidents of children possessed by an evil spirit. When
Jesus was ministering in the region of Tyre and Sidon a Caananite woman approached Him asking for
the healing of her little daughter. Mark used the di-
minutive form of "daughter" indicating that she was
a child. The mother was from a pagan culture but
was somewhat enlightened concerning the God of
Israel and from that minimal knowledge sought the
deliverance. The cause of the condition is not given
to us in the biblical account. But after testing the
woman's faith, Jesus healed her daughter by expelling the demon (Mark 7:24-30).

Another such incident occurred as Jesus came
down from the Mount of Transfiguration. He
found some of His disciples failing in their attempt

to cast out a spirit. Christ inquired of the father of the victim as to when this condition began. The father stated that the boy had been possessed since childhood.

How do children become possessed? They do not have long histories of deep sin nor have they engaged in deliberate communication with evil spirits. Is their condition inherited, as some claim, or are they victims of involuntary entrance of demons, as others teach? I would like to suggest a third possible explanation for the possession of children.

The activity of evil spirits was rampant across Palestine in the days of Jesus. Occult practices could be found among Jews who were not living according to the Torah. Greeks and Romans had taken up residence in the country and brought with them the animistic characteristics of their cultures. On the west coast of the land were the remnants of the Canaanites and the Phoenicians. These children, under the age of accountability (as indicated in the Greek) were no doubt exposed directly to animistic ceremonies. The intensity of such experiences could well pave the way for demon invasion.

Those cases of possession among very young children I have had contact with were all subject repeatedly to healing rituals where the spirits were implored to heal. The circumstances of the two cases mentioned in the New Testament may have been similar. Both children were victims of their animistic religious background. The issue of personal accountability is different with a small child. Parents must take accountability even as they did in the biblical accounts mentioned above. The people Christ delivered came to Him for help. The children He delivered were brought to Him by their parents.

Spiritual Mapping

Some modern missiologists have developed a methodology known as "spiritual mapping." Based on the concept of territorial spirits, it is a means of identifying the activity of certain spirits in a given geographical area. Charles Kraft compares this approach with the spies Moses sent into the land of promise.[1] The problem with that analogy is the absence of the kind of objective exploration of places and things in any effort to spy out the enemy's territory. It is totally subjective.

Of course, it can be agreed that evil spirits are entrenched and powerfully at work in some geographical areas more than others. The Spirit-filled believer will sense this evil presence and respond to it in terms of Christ's victory and the authority of His name. But the process of spiritual mapping raises the question of a legitimate source of information in order to do the mapping. Since the operation is invisible, it must be detected by outward evidences or by some means of communication either with an animist or the spirits.

Nothing in the Word of God even faintly suggests that God's servants should invade Satan's territory for information of any kind. If by observable facts we see extreme resistance to the gospel or widespread practices of witchcraft and other forms of satanic worship, or overt and numerous practices of wickedness, or oppressive spiritual darkness, it can be assumed that the powers of evil have a stronghold in that area. These kinds of observations are not a new idea. They have long been standard among those who do battle with the enemy for the glory of Christ.

The advocates of spiritual mapping speak of their methodology as a science. Science by its very nature and definition cannot deal with the supernatural. A clinical and/or scientific approach to demonic activity holds a strong potential for deception. The Church is dealing with the mystery of iniquity when she undertakes to do battle with the powers of hell. At every turn we meet the unexplainable and must flee to the arms of Christ and the shelter of His blood, the light of His truth. Nothing else will prevail against the enemy.

Detecting the Presence of Demons

The Christian doctrine of angelology teaches the existence of an order of intelligent beings called angels. They were created by God as free moral agents. Scripture testifies that a part of the angels rebelled against God their Creator and were by divine judgment expelled from heaven. These evil spirits (or evil angels) under the leadership of Satan have access to the earth.

Charles Hodge, renowned reformed theologian of the last century, in his *Systematic Theology* said, "As to the power and agency of these evil spirits, they are represented as being exceedingly numerous. As everywhere efficient, as having access to our world, and as operating in nature and the minds of men. . . ."[2] Hodge goes on to say that the evil angels like the good angels are invisible and cannot be detected by humans. He denies that humans could be conscious of the presence of evil spirits.

> . . . we are to be thankful to God for the unseen and unknowable ministry of the angels of light, and be on our guard and seek divine protection from the machinations of the spirits of evil. But of neither are we directly conscious, and to the

agency of neither can we with certainty refer any specific effect, if its occurrence admits of any other explanation.[3]

As cautious as Hodge was on the consciousness of men and women to spirit activity, he had to leave the door open in view of the fact that some events could not be otherwise explained. Hodge sees demon possession as an activity of evil spirits that is discernible by humans.

Some contemporary theologians raise the question: Can we in any way detect the presence and activity of the invisible evil spirits? The concern comes from the excessive claims of some who work in the field of deliverance ministry. The truth lies somewhere between the two extremes. If evil spirits (demons) can have such access to a human personality as is manifest in possession, it is reasonable to conclude that people can in certain circumstances be aware of and detect the presence and activity of demons. The activity in most cases of possession is so overt as to be obvious to any bystander. Certainly a discerning, Spirit-filled Christian would have an equal or greater awareness of the demonic activity.

If Christians are to put on the whole armor of God and do battle with the hosts of darkness, they must have some sense of where they are working and what they are doing. The New Testament does present a teaching that relates directly to this problem. The church in Corinth had many members saved out of the animistic religion of the Greeks. They were so familiar with demons that Paul warned them of the danger of knowingly participating in the table of demons. In his discussion of their spiritual gifts, Paul reminded them of the gift of discerning of spirits. The Anglican Greek scholar, Henry Alford, defines this gift as the power of distinguishing between the operation of the Spirit of God and the evil spirits.[4] The gift of discerning of spirits is critical to a church functioning in a culture given over to animistic practices.

Paul's teaching on discernment was given in the context of assembly gatherings and the use of the gifts of the Spirit in the assembly. But does this limit the exercise of the gift of discerning of spirits to church meetings only? It would not seem so, since encounters with the powers of darkness may occur apart from an assembly. If the Holy Spirit can enable a believer to discern the working of an evil spirit in the church, He could also enable him or her in any other situations where such a gift is needed.

Even without this gift, it is hardly conceivable that a true Christian could spend the night only a few feet away from a ceremony where direct traffic with evil spirits is taking place and have no consciousness of the presence of evil spirits. David Brainerd, early missionary to the North American Indians, relates his experience in the forests of Western Pennsylvania when he encountered a powerful shaman. Graphically describing the confrontation, Brainerd says,

> But of all the sights I ever saw around them, none appeared so frightful and so near akin to what is usually imagined of infernal powers, none ever expected such images of terror in my mind as the appearance of one who was a devout and zealous reformer or rather restorer of what he supposed was the ancient religion of the Indians.[5]

Brainerd describes the fear that attended their ceremony and goes on to tell of his later meeting with a more subdued shaman. Missionaries from around the world can confirm that experience.

Somewhere between spiritual mapping and a total lack of any sensitivity to evil spirits lies the truth. The practical value of being conscious of the enemy's presence and work is to alert the believer to immediate action by taking a stand for Christ. The word is plain: "Therefore submit to God. Resist the devil and he will flee from you" (James 4:7). When the "ruler of this world" was about to approach Jesus (John 14:30), He was alert to the fact. He expected His disciples to be as well.

The Essential Focus

The presence, power and activity of Satan and his demons are a reality. The church or individual that blocks out any awareness of this evil empire denies reality. While some may go overboard by seeing a demon behind every tree, the denial of the truth results in serious damage.

Fundamental to a sound ministry of deliverance is a sound theology of deliverance. Deliverance is not a scientific work but a supernatural one.

In 1959, A.W. Tozer wrote a masterful chapter on how to deal with the devil. He wisely points out that there is only a hairline between truth and superstition. Tozer offered this wise counsel to the Church:

> The scriptural way to see things is to set the Lord always before us, put Christ in the center of our vision, and if Satan is lurking around he will appear on the margin only and be seen as but a shadow on the edge of the brightness. It is always wrong to reverse this—to set Satan

in the focus of our vision and push God out to the margin. Nothing but tragedy can come of such inversion.[6]

Adherence to this theological premise will keep us from drifting toward the fanatic fringe in matters of spiritual warfare.

Endnotes

[1] Edward Rommen, ed., *Spiritual Power and Missions* (Pasadena, CA: William Carey Library, 1995), p. 132.

[2] Charles Hodge, *Systematic Theology*, Vol. 1 (Grand Rapids, MI: Eerdmans, 1952 edition), p. 644.

[3] Ibid., p. 645.

[4] Henry Alford, *Greek New Testament*, Vol. 3 (London: Deights, Bell and Co., 1871), p. 579.

[5] Jonathan Edwards, *Life of David Brainerd* (New York: American Tract Society, n.d.), pp. 173-174.

[6] A.W. Tozer, *Born after Midnight* (Camp Hill, PA: Christian Publications, 1989), p. 43.

CHAPTER NINE

The Church's New Battlefront

For the first time in the modern era, the Church in the West is faced with a sizeable population of people who worship evil spirits. The alarm has been sounded. This battle with strange gods will require a Spirit-filled Church armed with sound doctrine, the integrity of holiness and a view to the glory of God at His ultimate victory.

ANIMISM IS THE technical name for a belief system that sees spirits dwelling in all animate and inanimate objects. The followers of this system worship the spirits as their gods. Most animists believe in both good and evil spirits that require them to appeal to the so-called good ones and to appease the evil ones.

The Bible declares animism to be the worship of evil spirits. Such worship is sometimes called paganism and also polytheism. This growing world religion has long been an object of the Church's outreach concentrated mainly in Third World countries. In Asia, Africa and the Island World, animists number over 135 million.[1] However, that statistic does not include the millions of Muslims, Hindus and Buddhists who continue to pursue spirit worship and other animistic ways.

Dr. Ralph D. Winter, director of the U.S. Center for World Mission, reports that the Hindu world is the most implacable, demonically invaded part of the world.[2] Though Islam would like to impress the West with the idea that it is a highly philosophical and monotheistic religion, the hard facts reveal a strong undercurrent of occult and other animistic practices among Muslims all over the world. A visit to Thailand or Cambodia would soon convince the most skeptical that the followers of Buddha are also deeply into spirit worship.

In the past quarter century, a growing movement toward animism has developed in the so-called Christian countries of the West. In the United States, animists now number in the millions and Muslims are said to outnumber Methodists.[3] Over one-half million Buddhists and 1.26 million Hindus live in North America.[4] Added to these are millions of followers of the widespread New Age movement who are also engaged in animistic spirit worship.

Most of the animists in the United States are mainstream people. They have nice homes in nice suburbs, drive nice cars and enjoy the nice things the American economy affords. They are for the most part well educated and literate. The doctor who delivered my granddaughter is an outstanding East Indian who still follows his ancient faith though he drives a Mercedes and lives in an

$800,000 house. Apparently, none of these things has altered his or their belief system. It is easy to forget their spiritual darkness.

For the first time in the modern era, the Church in the West stands face-to-face with a sizeable population of people who worship evil spirits. Religious pluralism has become a fact of life. The Church can no longer evade or ignore this reality. The time has come to address the question: What must we do to ready ourselves to meet this new battlefront? We have sent our troops to the ends of the earth to fight the powers of darkness. Now we must fight this war on our own turf. What a glorious challenge it is to go to war to liberate souls rather than subjugate them!

The Biblical Foundation

One cannot deny the state of religious pluralism in our culture. The liberal church and secular humanists contend that all religions make some contribution to spirituality, therefore the Church should move toward a common religion made up of the best from each. Such a position betrays the fact that its promoters have set aside the revealed Word of God as the source of truth.

On the other hand, the evangelical Christian takes his stand with historic Christianity for the authority of Scripture. Both liberals and evangelicals believe in tolerance. The evangelicals' tolerance, as opposed to that of the liberals, is moderated by truth. The burning question is: What does the Bible say about God Almighty and His position on other gods?

Both the Old and New Testaments strictly forbid the worship of any other gods than the Most High God. The Most High God is the Creator of all things, the Sustainer of all things, the God who has revealed Himself in the Scriptures and in the incarnation of His Son, the Redeemer and the Sovereign Lord of history. The blessed Trinity is the only God to be worshiped. The psalmist said, "For the LORD Most High is awesome; He is a great King over all the earth" (Psalm 47:2). God warned Israel that if they served and worshiped other gods He would destroy them (1 Kings 9:6-7).

Russell H. Bowers, Jr., a missionary educator in Singapore, writes, "For the Christian, the first fundamental of faith is the existence of the transcendent yet personal God."[5] God is transcendent above all He has created. Because He is a personal God, He has spoken and has acted consistently with His perfect moral nature. The Most High God is the God of mercy, love and grace.

By comparison, all other gods are strange gods, with no real power to meet humanity's deepest need. The Bible tells of a time in the life of the patriarch Jacob when he moved to Bethel out of concern for the spiritual state of his family. He urged them to put away their foreign gods and worship only the true God (Genesis 35:2). The King James Version translates the phrase "foreign gods" as "strange gods." The Hebrew meaning infers something that is strange or foreign in the sense that it was unlawful for the people of God.[6] These false gods are strange in that they deny the true God and seek people to worship them in His place. Satan's sin was to place himself above God. He still persists in seeking worship from human beings. We know these things to be true because God has revealed them in His Word. The Bible plainly describes the reality of animism and condemns it.

Os Guinness in *The Dust of Death* says,

> The call to the Christian is twofold. Knowing the reality of these things in the context of the greater reality of God, we can have no time for the shallow, superficial stupidity of modern occultism where it is hoax. But where it is real, it stands as a challenge to God's character and man's freedom and it is time to demonstrate the greater power and genuine freedom that are ours in Christ.[7]

Only a fresh affirmation of bibical truth will

change how the Church deals with the current on-slaught of strange gods. The major reason for the culture's openness to this new breed of animism is the spiritual vacuum created by liberal Christianity and secular humanism. The battle requires a Spirit-filled Church armed with sound doctrine and the integrity of practical holiness.

The Victims of This Darkness

The devastating results of this recent resurgence of paganism came to me in the regular course of my pastoral duties.

One morning, as I sat in my study wading through the mail, my secretary advised me of an urgent telephone call. It was one of our deacon-esses on the line. She quickly shared her experience with a young mother who attended her neighbor-hood Bible study. What she described to me had all the earmarks of demonic activity.

That afternoon, the two of them came to my study. The young woman was attractive, intelli-gent and personable. She shared with me that she and her husband had recently accepted Christ and that subsequently things had taken a very ugly turn when she began to be plagued with illness and psychological problems. The medical doctors were perplexed and could find no pathological rea-sons for her symptoms.

At this point in the interview, I began to ask about her family and religious background. Vicky had grown up where witchcraft and the occult were routine. As a teenager she had, for a brief time, been involved with drugs. Out of that came a pregnancy, followed by an abortion. The young man she eventually married was a Satanist who practiced his evil arts in their home.

I began to discuss with her what the Scriptures said about witchcraft and the occult. We also talked about the manner in which Jesus dealt with demons. She began to comprehend the possibility that demons could be the cause of all her trouble. The next step was to take her through a renunciation of the evil practices in her past life and to ask God's forgiveness and cleansing.

After this preparation, I suggested we pray. Within minutes, she went into a coma. I tested the spirit. When it immediately denied that Christ had come in the flesh, we knew we were dealing with a case of demon possession.

Over the next hour, seven demons were cast out of this young mother. The spirits gave the following names: "family lineage, occult sickness, sexual impurity, guilt, suicide, murder." As each demon was cast out, she would convulse and froth at the mouth. After the last demon left, she sat up and began to praise the Lord. When she returned home, her husband was astounded at the change. The fear, darkness and sickness were gone.

Problems such as Vicky's are becoming all too commonplace in mainstream America.

I was preaching at a summer Bible conference where an executive secretary from a very prestigious firm came to the altar for counseling. Some deep bondage was tearing her life apart. Other ministers joined me. After a long session, we determined that demonic activity might be the cause of her anguish. Twenty-two demons were eventually expelled from this young woman. After she returned to her home church, her pastor and his wife followed up her case and later reported that the victory was real and lasting.

A thirty-eight-year-old man came to see me at the urging of his pastor. He shared the years of defeat and despair that had characterized his life to that point. He was at the time under discipline for causing problems in his local fellowship. For years he had not been able to hold a job for more than a few weeks. He showed a good understanding of doctrine, but had no capacity to live the Christian life. His family suffered much at his hand.

During the early part of the first session, he tried to defend himself, but God began to deal with his heart. It was then that he exposed the roots of his problem.

He had been raised in the church and after high school attended a Bible college to prepare for ministry. There he developed a pattern of breaking rules and creating conflicts with the faculty and administration. After one serious infraction, he was put on probation with some limitations on his activities. In an outburst of anger, he left the college and joined a cult, hoping to embarrass the school.

From the day of his baptism into this group, a dark and sinister force took hold of his life. The intervening years had come and gone with no improvement. He continued to leave a path of misery behind him wherever he went. It took a couple of sessions before he showed any brokenness. It was then that we discussed the possibility that his problem was of demonic origin.

A meeting was called with some church elders and ministers present. The manifesting demon did not want to respond to the question regarding Christ's coming in the flesh. Well over an hour went by before it answered in the negative. From that point, things began to break. A number of demons were cast out. The first gave its name as "false Jesus." Many of the demons were related to pseudo-religious experiences including a false gift of tongues. Over a period of weeks, all the evil spirits were expelled and the young man manifested a substantial change in appearance, action and attitude. Since then he has been able to hold a job and shows a marked difference in his life.

These accounts and hundreds like them blow away our old stereotypes about demon possession. It is not just a Third World phenomenon anymore. It happens in the towns and cities of mid-America and the victims are our neighbors. This is a wake-up call for the Church. Not only do we need to free the bound in the name of the Lord Jesus Christ, but also we must evangelize—or we will become the minority religion in America.

A Call to Renewal

The neglect of sound preaching and teaching on bibical demonology has left the evangelical Church vulnerable and unprepared for the situation that now confronts us. The Church is in a harvest field of rare opportunity. How can we be equipped for this opportunity? The answers are several.

A firm foundation must be laid by renewing the doctrine of demonology in its theological context. When this teaching is divorced from the whole of Christian theology, it becomes a methodology and takes a disproportionate place in the Church. I am not speaking of the emergence of some new trend, but the recovery of apostolic truth. Some years ago Merrill Unger, professor at Dallas Theological Seminary, saw the significance of a demonology related to the whole spectrum of truth. Unger said,

> From whatever angle biblical demonology is approached, whether it be the existence, the identity, the origin, the numbers or the organization of the demons, Scripture lays pre-eminent and continual stress on one central fact: Man requires deliverance and protection from these malignant destructive creatures.[8]

In the same chapter, Unger shows how demonology must dovetail with human depravity and redemption and the triumph of Jesus Christ. It is a biblical teaching that relates to every Christian in every age of Church history. It is related to the maturation and walk of every believer. No evangelism effort can hope to succeed without reference to this truth. The church that meets this new battlefront and wins is the church that internalizes the victory of Christ in its membership and then confronts the enemy with the whole armor of God.

Christ taught His disciples to pray, "And do not lead us into temptation, but deliver us from the evil one" (Matthew 6:13). This model prayer indicates the major concerns for which one ought to pray daily. That Jesus made the believer's conflict with the devil a matter of daily prayer puts spiritual warfare in its proper perspective. It is ongoing. It is real. It is not optional. One cannot say, "I do not want to be involved." Everyone is involved whether they know it or not. The victorious walk with Christ is down a path that leads through alien territory. Christians are to look to Christ for help in the two greatest contests of their lives—temptation and the devil's schemes to bring them into spiritual bondage.

The Christian is a soldier according to the apostle Paul. Good soldiers are fully consecrated to the cause of their Leader. They see Christ as the Captain of the Hosts of the Lord. As good soldiers, they lay aside all unnecessary impediments so that full attention may be on winning the war.

The conflict is not in a flesh-and-blood arena. It is *spiritual* warfare; therefore, no carnal weapon can be used. The weapons of our warfare are mighty through God (2 Corinthians 10:4). Enormous power is necessary for spiritual warfare. It takes the power of the resurrection to win this battle. The power that raised Jesus from the dead is greater than all the combined physical forces of the universe. That is the same power that saves the sinner, raises the dead in the coming rapture of God's people and becomes the empowerment of the believer for victory in the battle with the world, the flesh and the devil.

The Alert Has Been Sounded

More and more believers are seeing a relationship between the revival of paganism and the predicted signs of the end of the age and the second coming of Christ. Paul was convinced of the importance of being alert to the changes in satanic activity. In his letter to the church at Rome, he urged them to be spiritually awake and sensitized to the times. He said, "The night is far spent, the day is at hand. Therefore let us cast off the works of darkness, and let us put on the armor of light" (Romans 13:12). The context of this verse indicates Paul had in mind the conditions of the last days.

Twice is his letters to Timothy, Paul called attention to increased demonic activity in the end times. In the first reference, he said, "Now the Spirit expressly says that in latter times some will depart from the faith, giving heed to deceiving spirits and doctrines of demons" (1 Timothy 4:1). Inspired by the Holy Spirit, Paul predicted that demons would be active in spreading heresy in the Church as the time for Christ's return draws near.

The invasion of false teaching is already a battle line in the Church's war with the enemy. Satan is clever enough to know that the church that compromises the faith once delivered to the saints will be powerless. The devil has no doubt assigned the best minds among the powers of evil to seduce God's people with false teaching.

In Second Timothy, the last days are described as perilous times. Human behavior will reach an all-time low. Paul paints the picture of an ugly social scene characterized by perversion, selfishness, greed, self-indulgence, rebellion and the breakdown of the home. Demons are not mentioned here, but I believe it is self-evident that this level of wickedness has behind it, as instigator and perpetrator, the kingdom of darkness.

The acceleration of demonic activity in our time should not take us by surprise. The alert has been sounded. The present movement may be a forerunner of the times of the Antichrist when the ultimate manifestation of demon power will sweep over the world during the Great Tribulation. The book of Revelation tells of the release of hordes of demons having as their mission the gathering of the nations to the Battle of Armageddon (Revelation 16:13-16). The spirit of Antichrist has been at work since the days of the apostles (1 John 4:3).

No study of spiritual warfare is complete that omits the eschatalogical dimension of the subject. On the basis of prophetic Scripture, it is reasonable to assume that the widespread and overt activity of demonic forces is a call to watchfulness on the part of the Church. Christ exhorts us to watch for we do not know the hour of our Lord's return.

This alert is also a call to action. Satan is working a strategy of deception to ensnare the Church in a scheme to make herself attractive to the world by being as much like the world as she dare be. The church that follows that plan is helpless in battle against powers of evil. To confront evil and the intelligence behind the evil in these perilous times, God's people must be pure, separated from the world and ablaze with the fire of Pentecost.

The Nature of Spiritual Warfare

The fall of Lucifer and the angels who followed him introduced enmity in the universe. The fallen angels became demons and their fallen leader became the devil. The hostility of these wicked beings is directed toward God and the people of God. Satan and his forces have determined to make "war on the saints." The Scriptures suggest that God has permitted the ongoing pressure of the enemy in order to test the allegiance of His people. Satan had asked that Peter be sifted as wheat. The extent of the test would be so great that Jesus promised Peter He would pray for him (Luke 22:31-32). In the Old Testament, the book of Job relates a similar account.

Satan and the demons are utterly powerless before God. They work now as usurpers, attempting to claim ground that does not belong to them. The death and resurrection of Christ dealt the final blow to the kingdom of darkness. The finished work of Christ provides all that is needed for the believer to overcome the devices, attacks and threats of the powers of evil.

These things being true, the basic spiritual issue with regard to the Christian's involvement in spiritual warfare is total surrender to Christ. There must be a full-heart allegiance to the Lord Jesus. No amount of training or instruction can make up for the weaknesses of an unyielded life.

Spiritual warfare deals with everything from fending off temptation to a full-scale encounter with the powers of darkness. Therefore every Christian to some degree is engaged in this war. Each believer must learn to apply the glorious victory of Christ in his or her own encounters with the enemy. It is in these struggles we prove the power of the indwelling Christ over all the power of the enemy. Those who allow frequent defeats in their personal encounters with the devil will find it difficult to engage in spiritual warfare at the corporate level.

The health and ministry of the Church are constant targets of the powers of evil. The armies of hell are unrelenting in their battle to hinder the work of world evangelism. Satan does not readily give up the control of the millions he has held for so long.

Spirit-energized intercession is vital in breaking down the strongholds of the enemy. Prayer lies alongside the armor of God as an essential instrument in our war with Satan. Evangelism that does not anticipate the resistance of the unseen powers of evil is bound to fail. True evangelism is not marketing—it is war. The relationship of spiritual warfare and the evangelization of the world can no longer be ignored.

A Mind-set for the Battle

No doubt some Christians will take the position that confronting this new level of demonic activity in our culture is depressing and unrealistic. They may even label it fanaticism. But I believe we can do nothing less. Ours is not the first generation of the Church called upon to take such a stand.

When Martin Luther stood firm for the gospel of Christ against church and government, all hell broke loose. His life was in danger and he suffered the personal attacks of the devil. But Martin Luther stood unmoved on the sure ground of Christ's victory. Out of his experience he wrote the hymn, "A Mighty Fortress Is Our God." One verse of that hymn describes the mind-set the Church

might assume as she takes on the new battlefront
of mushrooming animism in our culture:

> And though this world, with devils filled,
> Should threaten to undo us,
> We will not fear, for God hath willed
> His truth to triumph through us:
> The Prince of Darkness grim—
> We tremble not for him;
> His rage we can endure,
> For lo, his doom is sure,
> One little word shall fell him.

The attitude of the reformer was shaped by his
faith. He did not question for a moment the complete victory of Christ over Satan and all his demons. The roar of the lion sent no fear to his heart.
Jesus Christ won at Calvary and Luther knew it. So
should we.

The encounter with the powers of evil in Christ's
name should be a triumphant and joyful undertaking. Whether the strategy takes the form of apolo-
getics, evangelism, intercessory prayer or exorcism,
let the soldiers of Christ arise, all armed for battle,
and carry out our standing orders without fear.

The good soldier of Christ has the God-given
ability to differentiate the people from the battle.
True spiritual warfare is never with people, but

with the demons who attack or control people. To be successful in reaching animists, Christian workers will have to get rid of racial prejudice and every other unhealthy attitude. Our mind-set must be that of love and deep compassion.

Conclusion

They are already standing at the doorstep— animists from every part of the world, Native Americans still practicing traditional religions and an unnumbered host of citizens who follow New Age religions. The aggregate of all these peoples forms one of the largest mission challenges in the world.

The churches that thrust in the sickle and reap this harvest will be the churches that believe Christ to be the same yesterday, today and forever. They will believe that even now, from His throne in glory just as when He walked on earth, He is able to dislodge the forces of evil.

The ancient scourge of demon possession is as real in modern America as it was when Christ was upon earth. The answer to this terrible human blight is found only in the power of Christ. He has provided the commission, the equipment and the authority to do this work.

Every incident of deliverance from demon possession is a microcosm of the coming kingdom

glory when Christ will have laid every enemy at
His feet.

The glory of God. That is the primary and final
purpose of deliverance. The ministry of deliverance—in your life and mine—will take on a new
and exciting perspective when viewed in the light
of the glory of God.

Even so come, Lord Jesus.

Endnotes

[1] *Encyclopedia Americana,* Vol. 1 (Danbury, CT: Grolier,
Inc., 1989), p. 888.

[2] Ralph D. Winter, *Mukti Mission Magazine*, May 1995, p.
2.

[3] David F. Wells, *No Place for Truth* (Grand Rapids, MI:
Eerdmans, 1993), p. 262.

[4] David Jeremiah, *Invasion of Other Gods* (Dallas, TX:
Word, 1995), p. 29.

[5] Russel H. Bowers, Jr., "Defending God before the Buddhist Emptiness," *Bibliotheca Sacra,* Vol. 154, Oct-Dec.
1997, p. 402.

[6] William Wilson, *Old Testament Word Studies* (McLean,
VA: MacDonald Publishers, n.d.), p. 422.

[7] Os Guinness, *The Dust of Death* (Downers Grove, IL: In-
terVarsity Press, 1973), p. 311.

[8] Merrill Unger, *Biblical Demonology* (Wheaton, IL: Scripture Press, 1973), p. 215.

Demon Possessed or Demonized?

I N THE PAST decade or more the terms "demon possession" and "demon possessed" have been called in question by some scholars. Merrill F. Unger of Dallas Theological Seminary and C. Fred Dickason of Moody Bible Institute are among the evangelicals who believe "demon possession" to be an incorrect translation of the participle *daimonizomenos*.

This participle is used in the Greek New Testament some twelve times for the condition traditionally called "demon possession." Both of the above scholars prefer to translate the participle as "demonized." They offer the following reasons for their position:

1. The term "demon possession" does not appear in the Bible. Unger says that this term originated with Flavius Josephus, a first-century Jewish historian.

2. When the participle is translated "demon possession," the word "possession" implies ownership. Demons own nothing.

3. The etymological analysis of *daimonizomenos* is summarized as a "demon-caused passivity." It is concluded that demonization pictures a demon controlling a somewhat passive person.

4. The term "demon possession," according to Dickason, is confusing and misused (see Bibliography).

In response to the above arguments, let us look at the term "demon possession" in the light of historic theology.

The term has been in use for as long as the Church has had literature. While Edersheim maintains the term came into the theological vocabulary of the Church from the writings of Josephus, this is only a theory. It is also possible that it came by way of apostolic tradition. The real point is not its origin but its meaning and its long usage by all branches of the Church.

Demon possession has been studied and defined by some of the best minds of the Church for almost two millennia. It is significant to see the consistency of Bible translators in translating the above Greek participle into English. Every English translation done by a team of qualified scholars has used "possessed by a demon." This reflects the best thinking over the last four centuries.

Before leaving the word "possession," it might be well to consult the English dictionary for its meaning: "Possession: The act of having or taking into control. Control or occupancy of property without regard to ownership." Ownership follows the above meanings which means the term "possession" in its secular meaning can refer to controlling or occupying without ownership. Control appears to be more critical than ownership in the above definition of possession. The third definition given by the dictionary reads, "A domination by something (an evil spirit, a passion, or an idea)."[1]

The argument that "possession" is the wrong word because it implies ownership does not hold up against the dictionary definition of possession. The dictionary uses the illustration of a ball. The usage in the matter of a team "possessing" the ball does not infer their ownership of the ball but their control of the ball. From the standpoint of the English language, the expression "demon possession" is an acceptable equivalent of "possessed by a demon."

The word "possession" is a noun form as over against the adjective form "possessed." The fact that theological language uses the noun form rather than the adjective is of no real consequence either linguistically or theologically.

The word "demonize" is found in the English dictionary as a derivation of "demon." The dictionary does not place the definition of "demonize" under "demoniac" where it defines the condition of one under demon control. In other words, "demonized" is not to be used to describe persons under demonic control.

The words "demonize" or "demonization" as used by Unger and Dickason are not translations but transliterations from the Greek like the word "baptize." It is open to more than one meaning. "Demonize" has no established theological meaning. Each writer defines the term as he sees it. That being so, one has to ask why "demonization" is preferable to "demon possession." What does it say that is more accurate biblically?

The ambiguity of the word "demonize" is creating confusion in the field of deliverance ministry. Both Unger and Dickason have defined "demonize" clearly from their point of view and that point of view relates to their perception of the possibility of a believer being possessed or, to use their term, "demonized." Both of the above scholars fall back to the traditional term when attempting to focus their definition of "demonize." Unger says, "Although severe demon influence resembles demon possession, it is never the same. In demon possession one or more evil spirits dwell in a person's body as their house and take complete possession of it at times."[2] This is a traditional definition of demon possession.

One must agree with Unger that demon possession correctly used refers to any case where a demon indwells and controls a human being. Not every writer who uses "demonize" has a clear understanding of its meaning. Some in the ministry of deliverance use "demonization" to redefine the whole concept of demon possession.

One popular deliverance ministry, in dealing with issues of believers being demon possessed, notes in their manual:

> If you mean, can a Christian be totally owned by a demon or Satan, you cannot be totally owned by Satan or a demon. The Bible does not use the term "demon possessed" which does imply total ownership. The New Testament considers them squatters or invaders of territory

that is not theirs. . . . The word "demon
possessed" correctly translated means
"demonized" which is a hold evil spirit(s)
have on a man in any shade or degree.[3]

This quotation essentially denies demon possession as understood by the Church across the centuries. It claims that a person is not possessed but
invaded by demons or attacked by demons. This is
a redefinition of the condition described in the
New Testament without regard for the plain statements of the Greek text. It appears to be carefully
crafted to deal with the theological problem of a
Christian being demon possessed.

John Wimber, the founder of the Vineyard
Movement, calls the traditional term "demon possession" an unbiblical concept. Wimber's concept
of "demonize" has a number of theological problems. He broadens the term to take in all forms of
demonic activity upon humans.

The word "demonize" is not only used by sound
scholars, but also by those who are creating an innovative concept of power encounter. The ambiguity of the word "demonize" makes it possible to
totally redefine the doctrine of demonology. Conrad Murrell in his book *Practical Demonology* gives
an example of such a redefinition:

> The word *daimonizomai* does not mean to be possessed or owned in the sense we understand possession. It simply means to be demonized or to be in some way affected by a demon. . . . It is wrong to say that a person is demon possessed simply because he has demons in his body.[4]

Murrell denies the traditional theological view of demon possession and does so on the basis of translating *daimonizomai* as "demonized." He later admits that the demoniac of Gadara was possessed in the traditional sense. The question must then be raised: When does *daimonizomai* mean "demon possession" and when does it mean "affected by a demon"? So far as I can discover, *daimonizomai* is never used of any other condition than possession.

The studies in this book are devoted to actual cases of demon possession and the use of the biblical process of exorcism. People that are not possessed but only troubled by evil spirits need prayer and counsel to liberate them. They must also learn to renounce the spirits. The failure to do so could eventually result in demon possession. The ministry of deliverance encompasses both of these methods of encountering the enemy—prayer/counsel and exorcism—and bringing about the freedom of the victim.

Endnotes

[1] These quotes are taken from *Merriam Webster's Collegiate Dictionary*, 10th ed. (Springfield, MA: Merriam-Webster, 1993), p. 909.

[2] Merrill Unger, *Demons in Today's World* (Wheaton, IL: Tyndale House, 1984), p. 113.

[3] *Lighthouse Procedure Manual* (Minneapolis: Lighthouse Ministries, n.d.), p. 11.

[4] Conrad Murrell, *Practical Demonology* (Bently, LA: Saber Publishers, 1982), p. 54.

Territorial Spirits

TIMOTHY M. WARNER is credited with being the first missiologist to use the term "territorial spirits." The concept has become popular in the current prayer movement and among those who carry on a deliverance ministry both in America and overseas. Imprecise in his definition of this term, he maintains that territorial demons are assigned to every geo-political unit in the world. The primary scriptural reference for this claim is Daniel 10:10-21.

Careful study needs to be given to this passage. It does reveal an important reality regarding the activity of demons. While in a prolonged time of prayer, Daniel was visited by an angel who made known to him the reason for the delay in answering his prayer. The angel revealed that he had been in a twenty-one-day battle with the prince of the kingdom of Persia and finally prevailed with the assistance of the angel Michael.

The angel told Daniel that when he departed he expected to encounter another power he called the prince of Greece (Daniel 10:20). It is evident the two princes mentioned here are very powerful spirit beings aligned with evil and resistant to God and His people. The demons are no doubt a part of the hierarchy of spiritual powers mentioned by Paul in Ephesians 6:12. Warner and many others call these two princes "territorial spirits." By that they mean their activity is associated with a geographical location. The question is: Does that theory hold up under careful study of the Scripture text?

Were these demons assigned to a geographical territory or were they assigned to a political system? The answer to that question lies in the context of the whole book of Daniel. The prophet had, prior to this occasion, been given a vision of the times of the Gentiles. Subsequent visions filled in the details of a series of powerful Gentile rulers who would achieve control of the world. God described these rulers as "beasts" with dark and sinister notions of morals, ethics and religion. These empires were to be enemies of the God of the Bible and His people Israel. The vision in Daniel 10:11ff established the idea that a malignant spiritual force was behind these empires. The emphasis, I believe, is on the system rather than the geographical territory.

Daniel did not do battle with the prince of Persia. It was the angel who fought this wicked power. It was a battle in the heavenlies between angels and demons. The spiritual turmoil was brought on by the intercessory prayers of Daniel. This passage details a real power encounter, but it can hardly be equated with what is now called "encounter with territorial spirits."

The Scripture offers no example of this kind of battle between believers and any extraordinarily malignant powers. Daniel seemed content to leave this battle with the angels and to devote his energy to confession and intense intercessory prayer.

Paul understood spiritual warfare as a spiritual battle. It was not against flesh and blood and, it might be inferred from this statement, not against specific geographic locations, even though demonic activity may go on in a given location. The focus of attack must be on the spiritual dominion, rule or control. There does not appear to be any biblical support for concentrating spiritual warfare on geographic locations. The Scriptures give no examples from the ministry of Christ or His apostles of any power encounter that was focused on specific areas. Therefore it would seem that the teaching of territorial spirits does not rest on clear biblical statements.

Some who hold to the concept of territorial spirits believe Jesus had this in mind when He spoke of Satan as a "strong man" (Matthew 12:28-29). Christ was speaking about the authority required to expel demons and asserted that He cast demons out by the Holy Spirit. The Pharisees accused Him of casting them out by the power of Beelzebub, the ruler of the demons. Christ showed the absurdity of their accusation through the story of a strong man who held his house secure so that no one could enter and plunder his goods. To get that which the strong man held in his power, he would have to be bound. Only then could his house be easily plundered. The point of the illustration is the power to bind the strong man, not his location.

Other verses that are cited to support the concept of territorial spirits are Galatians 4:3, 9. In these two verses the apostle Paul speaks of the believer's former state as being in bondage to the "elements of the world." The Greek word here translated "elements" is *stocheia* and is used again by Paul in Colossians 2:8, 20 and by the writer of Hebrews in Hebrews 5:12 where it is tranlated as "principle" each time. *Stoicheia* was also frequently used with regard to education and as a mathematical term. The root meaning of *stoicheia* is "to place in a row." The alphabet is a *stoicheia*. Plato used the word to designate the elements that make up the world.

During the 1930s some scholars concluded that *stoicheia* referred to angelic powers whose duty it was to preside over all natural happenings. That interpretation was largely rejected, for it failed to take into account that the emphasis of the text is upon philosophical elements rather than natural elements.

Those who see *stoicheia* as meaning territorial spirits run into the same difficulty. The illustration Paul uses makes reference to guardians and stewards in Galatians 4:2, but this does not require that the elements in verse 3 be personalities. *Stoicheia* is not used anywhere in the New Testament to speak of such. R.C.H. Lenski, professor of New Testament Greek and the author of a set of Greek commentaries on the entire New Testament, says of this theory of interpreting *stoicheia* as personalities,

> These *stoicheia* need not be persons so as to match the guardians and stewards of the illustration who are persons; for the point of the illustration is the fact that

the young heir is really under those who
are far beneath him. So the Old Testament believers were placed under material, earthly things that were beggarly,
indeed all of them far beneath these believers.[1]

Lenski makes the point that the idea of making
the *stoicheia* strong personalities does not fit Paul's
illustration.

Without a question there are powerful demons
in the organizational structure mentioned in Ephesians 6:12 and these powers are assigned to rule
the fallen cosmic system we call the world. To give
these spirits any name other than those found in
Scripture is unwarranted. By calling some of them
"territorial spirits" the inference is made that their
location can be known to believers, thus enabling
them to go to the exact site and bind or expel the
spirits.

This teaching has had a significant impact on
how some people perceive spiritual warfare. It has
produced a number of innovative methodologies in
the field of deliverance ministry, some of which
cause confusion. The means by which these locations are found are questionable. Some locations
have been supposedly identified by interviewing
demons. Others are located by asking the people of

the locality what the spirit-centers might be. This is all very subjective. It should be remembered that the demons are extremely deceptive.

I know of one group which had determined that a powerful demon was in control of their city and that the Christians should bind this demon and cast it out. The hoped-for result was that crime, violence, sex sins and other evils would be cleaned up. The end of that endeavor was nothing but a spiritual disaster.

I was once sent to deal with a church divided over extremes related to territorial spirits. One group in the church had determined that a number of powerful demons had taken up residence in the church and were hindering revival. They began long sessions of binding and loosing going from pew to pew. By the time I arrived, they had covered supposedly about half of the pews. The result of their effort was a divided church and a group of very disillusioned people.

Endnotes

[1] R.C.H. Lenski, *The Interpretation of Saint Paul's Epistles to the Galatians to the Ephesians to the Philippians* (Columbus, OH: The Wanburg Press, 1937), p. 196.

The Generational
Transmission of Demons

A NUMBER OF evangelicals have taken the position that demons are sometimes passed down in families from one generation to another. It is assumed that an ancestor has made a pact with the powers of darkness and consequently his or her children down to the fourth generation may inherit a controlling demon or demons. Much of this teaching is based on information given by demons and case studies.

The Scriptures which they cite in support of the generational transmission of spirits is Exodus 20:5: "You shall not bow down to them nor serve them [meaning other gods]. For I, the LORD your God, am a jealous God, visiting the iniquity of the fathers upon the children to the third and fourth generations of those who hate Me. . . ." The issue in this text is not demon possession but iniquity. To worship idols and/or other gods is a sin, and it is sin that the law deals with. Of course, the sin mentioned here can open the human personality to demonic invasion, but it cannot be concluded that all who worship idols are demon possessed. The Scripture does not say that God will visit demonic control on the subsequent generations of idolaters. It says He will visit the iniquity of the father on the next generations. This is consistent with the biblical understanding of judgment and retribution. If the second, third and fourth generations become possessed of evil spirits, it will be due to their strong affinity toward the sins of their father.

Kurt Koch writes about the phenomenon of inherited psychological disorders and sicknesses such as depression. His case studies show many instances of exposure to demonic activity from previous generations, but does not present a convincing case that demons are inherited. He does mention the possibility of inheriting the tendency toward the occult. All of these conclusions rest on psychiatric or psychological studies which provide no biblical foundation for the idea that demons are transmitted to subsequent generations in some families.[1]

The danger in this teaching is the unbiblical notion that some people inherit at birth something more than depravity. Nothing in Scripture suggests such a possibility. The Exodus passage is speaking clearly of a divine judgment that follows the sin of idolatry up to the fourth generation. A part of that retribution is the wicked influences that shape the lives of the next generations.

But each generation stands accountable for its own sins (Ezekiel 18:19-32). When Moses interceded for the children of those who disobeyed God and refused to enter the land of promise, he appealed to God for mercy and made reference to Exodus 20:5: "The LORD is longsuffering and abundant in mercy, forgiving iniquity and transgression; . . . visiting the iniquity of the fathers on the children to the third and fourth generation" (Numbers 14:18). Moses pled with God to pardon the sins of His people. God responded by saying that the wicked generation would perish, but the next generation would be blessed. The biblical record shows how wonderfully that next generation followed the Lord. They both entered and conquered the land of promise and walked with God in spite of what their parents had been. The teaching here is accountability for sin; that truth must always be central in the ministry of deliverance.

However, it should not be overlooked that

knowing about the involvement of ancestors in the occult is valuable to any given case of deliverance. Such important information can be secured without interviewing the demons or assuming the inheritance of demons.

Those who hold to the position that demons are transmitted in families from one generation to the next have yet to prove their stand from Scripture. There is no doubt that influence from occult parents or grandparents is a factor in some cases of possession, but that does not give license to draw conclusions that cannot be supported by Scripture. However, exposure to the occult and involvement by occult family members does sometimes pave the way for demon invasion. Still, that is far different than inheriting the demon or demons.

Endnotes

[1] Kurt Koch, *Christian Counseling and Occultism* (Grand Rapids, MI: Kregel Publications, 1981), pp. 138-139.

Bibliography

Arnold, Clinton E. *Ephesians Power and Magic*. Grand Rapids: Baker Book House, 1992.

Bailey, Keith M. *Divine Healing: The Childrens' Bread*. Camp Hill, PA: Christian Publications, Inc., 1977.

Birch, George A. *The Deliverance Ministry*. Beaverlodge, AB: Horizon House, 1988.

Blumhardt, Johann. *Blumhardt's Battle: A Conflict with Satan*. Translated by Frank S. Boshold, New York: Thomas Lowe, 1970. (The book was originally published in Germany in 1850.)

Brooks, Thomas. *Precious Remedies against Satan's Devices*. Evansville, IN: Sovereign Grace Publishers, 1960 Reprint.

Brown, Robert. *Demonology and Witchcraft*. London: John F. Shaw and Company, 1889.

Cuccaro, Elio, editor. *Alliance Academic Review*. Camp Hill, PA: Christian Publications, Inc., 1996.

Chafer, Lewis Sperry. *Satan, His Motives and Methods*. Grand Rapids: Zondervan Publishing House, 1977. (Original 1914.)

_____. *Demon Experiences in Many Lands*. Chicago: Moody Press, 1960.

Dickason, C. Fred. *Angels Elect and Evil*. Chicago: Moody Press, 1975.

_____. *Demon Possession and the Christian*. Wheaton: Crossway Books, 1987.

Dufrene, Phil and Elford, L.W. *Out of the Snare of the Devil*, Prince Albert: Northern Canada Evangelical Mission, 1987.

Gilpin, Richard. *Daemonologia Sacra or a Treatise of Satan's Temptations*. Minneapolis, MN: Klock and Klock, 1982.

Gordon, S.D. *Quiet Talks about the Tempter*. New York: Fleming & Revel, 1910.

Gray, James. *Spiritism and the Fallen Angels*. New York: Fleming & Revel, 1920.

Jeremiah, David L. *Invasion of the Other Gods*. Dallas: Word Publishing, 1995.

Knapp, Martin Wells. *Impressions*. Cincinnati: God's Revivalist Press, n.d.

Koch, Kurt. *Christian Counseling and Occultism*. Grand Rapids: Kregel Publications, 1981.

_____. *Between Christ and Satan*. Grand Rapids: Kregel Publications, 1961.

_____. *Occult Bondage and Deliverance*. Grand Rapids: Kregel, n.d.

Larkin, Clarence. *The Spirit World*. Published by the author, 1921.

Needham, Mrs. George C. *Angels and Demons*. Philadelphia: American Baptist Publications, 1895.

MacMillan, John A. *The Authority of the Believer*. Camp Hill, PA: Christian Publications, Inc., 1997.

Meade, Russel. *Victory over Demons Today*. Wheaton: Christian Life Publications, 1962.

Nevius, John L. *Demon Possession*. Grand Rapids: Kregel Publications, 1968.

Nordmo, J.M. *Demons Despoiled*. London: China Inland Mission, 1958.

Pemberton, G.H. *Earth's Earliest Ages*. London: Hodder and Stoughton, 1884.

Pink, Arthur W. *Satan and His Gospel*. Swengel, PA: Reiner Publications. n.d.

Schwarze, C. Theodore. *The Program of Satan*. Chicago: Good News Publishers, 1947.

Soltau, T. Stanley. *In the Enemy's Territory*. Published by the author, 1969 (Soltau was a Presbyterian missionary).

Rommen, Edward, editor. *Spiritual Power and Missions*. Pasadena: William Carey Library, 1995.

Unger, Merril F. *Biblical Demonology*. Wheaton: Scripture Press, 1952.

_____. *Demons in the World Today*. Wheaton: Tyndale House, 1984.

Warner, Timothy M. *Spiritual Warfare*. Wheaton: Crossway Books, 1991.

White, Levi. *The Borderland of the Supernatural*. Chicago: Christian Witness Company, 1905.

Other books by Keith M. Bailey

Divine Healing—The Children's Bread
Servants in Charge
Christ's Coming and His Kingdom